Victorians

Victorians

**Ian Roberts and
Brian Moses**

 David Fulton Publishers

David Fulton Publishers Ltd
2 Park Square, Milton Park, Abingdon, Oxon, OX14 4RN

Transferred to Digital Printing 2009

www.fultonpublishers.co.uk

First published in Great Britain in 2005 by David Fulton Publishers

David Fulton Publishers is a division of Granada Learning, part of ITV plc.

British Library Cataloguing in Publication Data
A catalogue record for this book is available from the British Library.

ISBN 1-84312-180-8

Designed and typeset by Kenneth Burnley, Wirral, Cheshire

Publisher's Note
The publisher has gone to great lengths to ensure the quality of this reprint
but points out that some imperfections in the original may be apparent.

Contents

Introduction

A common concern expressed by primary school teachers is that pressure exerted on curriculum time by factors such as the National Literacy Strategy (NLS), National Numeracy Strategy (NNS) and discrete subject teaching has had a detrimental effect on creativity and enjoyment.

Word and sentence level tasks have tended to swamp opportunities for longer pieces of creative writing. Furthermore, subjects taught in isolation have resulted in lost opportunities for primary schoolchildren to appreciate links between them.

In the DFE publication *Excellence and Enjoyment*, some of these problems appear to be acknowledged. Schools are reminded that NLS materials can be adapted to meet the individual needs of schools and that the schemes published by the Qualifications and Curriculum Authority (QCA) are optional. A further crucial reminder is also given as follows:

> There is no requirement for subjects to be taught discretely – they can be grouped or taught through projects. If strong enough links are created between subjects, pupils' knowledge and skills can be used across the curriculum.

The aim of this book is to provide stimulating historical source material linked to enjoyable, purposeful and challenging language activities aimed primarily for children in Key Stage 2 of the National Curriculum.

Resources have been chosen to fulfil two requirements:

1. For their diversity and interest in relation to the historical theme being studied.

2. To encourage creative responses that allow the development and application of literacy skills.

Connections, too, can be made between past and present – linking what we know now with what we find out about the past, linking who we are now and how we live today with the thoughts and deeds of our ancestors. It is about searching for clues and making comparisons between what was and what is now.

Are there links, for example, between the advertisements in Victorian newspapers and those found in 'ad mags' today? Can children discover similar sorts of advertisements – want ads, lonely hearts, lost and found, offers of employment, etc.?

The anthology material makes similar connections. How does school today compare with the descriptions in Dickens' books? Similarly with conditions of work and the way that Sunday is spent.

The photocopiable source material and suggested activities provide rich and varied opportunities to write in a wide range of genres. In addition, they present opportunities for speaking and listening, activities involving drama and further creative work. The suggested tasks can be used flexibly according to individual circumstances and specific needs of children.

Examples of usage include:

- Shared writing tasks with the teacher modelling a particular genre within the literacy hour.

- As additional tasks for more sustained writing outside the literacy hour.

- Tasks for small-group work. Children can list important facts or issues and present findings to the class. A 'panel of experts' could research an area of source materials. The rest of the class could draw up a list of twenty questions that could be put to the panel.

- Tasks for independent writing, the outcomes of which could be used for formative and summative assessment purposes.

- Exploration of different genres: diary entries could be rewritten as news reports or letters.

- Tasks aimed at challenging talented and more able pupils by providing greater breadth and depth of learning through the provision of a wider variety of opportunities.

- Homework activities.

- As supplementary material to extend children's learning beyond the National Curriculum programmes of study.

The source materials in this book provide opportunities for children to view material that was first seen by the Victorians themselves. They have been chosen to develop children's interest in, and understanding of, aspects of Victorian life including health, education, entertainment, employment, social expectations, technology, advertising and domestic life.

Some of the featured extracts are taken from newspapers published during the reign of Queen Victoria or are drawn from popular journals such as *Punch* and *The Illustrated London News*. Other material is taken from Victorian school log books and from *Mrs Beeton's Book of Household Management* (Mrs Beeton, 1836–65, is best known for her writing on cookery, and her book *Household Management* was first published in parts between 1859 and 1860 in a women's magazine).

While most sources are self-explanatory, readers may be unfamiliar with *Enquire Within Upon Everything*, published by Houlston and Sons, London. The 1884 edition used for our purposes was the 'carefully revised sixty-ninth edition'. The editor's explanation of the range and purpose of the volume was as follows:

> WHETHER YOU WISH TO MODEL A FLOWER IN WAX; TO STUDY THE RULES OF ETIQUETTE; TO SERVE A RELISH FOR BREAKFAST OR SUPPER; TO PLAN A DINNER FOR A LARGE PARTY OR A SMALL ONE; TO CURE A HEADACHE; TO MAKE A WILL; TO GET MARRIED; TO BURY A RELATIVE; WHATEVER YOU WISH TO DO, MAKE OR ENJOY, PROVIDED YOUR DESIRE HAS RELATION TO THE NECESSITIES OF DOMESTIC LIFE, I HOPE YOU WILL NOT FAIL TO ENQUIRE WITHIN.

Organisation

This book contains two main sections.

The first contains photocopiable source materials. Each source document is accompanied by short background notes and suggested activities.

In most cases, it is envisaged that teachers will introduce children to the source materials and provide opportunities for discussion of the suggested activities. An alternative approach might be to challenge more able children to work with the materials independently.

The second section of the book provides a collection of further source materials where children can read extracts that both complement and support material in the first section of the book. The descriptions of school life from Dickens and the account of a beating at Eton, for example, can be used alongside the section on 'Misbehaving Pupils'.

Part 1

Source materials and activities

'Now is the time to buy one!'

Stimulus material

- Cartoons, pictures and advertisements for inventions.

Background

Thousands of inventions were sent to the Patent Office during Victorian times. Some of these were manufactured and sold commercially while others, such as a walking stick that could be converted into a step ladder to escape attacks from angry dogs, just remained as fanciful ideas. The cartoon from an 1868 edition of *Punch* pokes fun at the idea of producing labour-saving devices. Advertisements for cheap products sometimes had hidden extras. If you read the bicycle advertisement carefully you will see that brakes are five shillings extra!

Suggested activities

Look at these pictures of gadgets and inventions. Imagine that your job is to sell one of them. You may need to take this invention from door to door. Your salary is dependent on your success! Think about what you will say and the questions that your potential customers may ask. Try to draw attention to all the good points of the invention and how it will benefit your customer if they buy one. They may notice drawbacks to the design of the product. How will you respond to these comments? (You will not sell many if you agree!) When you are ready, find a partner. Take turns in taking on the role of the salesperson and the potential customer. Act out your conversations. Write out your conversations in the form of a play script.

Extension activity

- Aim to design a device or gadget that can help or entertain people. Perhaps it could help children with some of their chores at home or school, or maybe you have a good idea for a toy or game. Think about techniques for interesting others in your product.

CALL IT A TOY, INDEED! WHY, OUR INGENIOUS FRIEND, GLIMMER, HAS A RUN BEFORE BREAKFAST, AND GRINDS HIS COFFEE AND CHURNS HIS BUTTER WITH THE GREATEST EASE.

SCIENCE IN THE POULTRY-YARD.

No, gentle reader, you are mistaken. This is simply a little stamping attachment invented by our old friend Rott, by which a person purchasing eggs can tell to the minute when they were laid. The upper picture shows the attachment, and the lower the result.

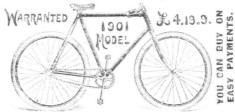

How (not) to speak Cockney

Cockney was a name given to people who were born within earshot of Bow Bells in London.

Stimulus material

- Cockney sweeps cartoon: *Punch,* 2 May 1863.
- Examples of Cockney speech: *Enquire Within Upon Everything*.
- Examples of Cockney rhyming slang, collected from Londoners.

Background

Before television and radio, there were many more regional dialects and variations in the way in which people spoke. However, 'polite society' in Victorian times was keen to encourage people to speak 'properly'.

Examples of 'incorrect speech' were published in *Enquire Within Upon Everything* and advice was given on correct methods.

Cockney rhyming slang appears to have been in use long before Victorian times. Some writers suggest that it was used extensively in Victorian London. These days, thanks to a popular television soap opera, some people appear to be adopting dialect and slang from the east end of London.

Suggested activities

- Speak like a Victorian Cockney! Act out the short conversations between Cockneys from the *Punch* cartoon and from the pages of *Enquire Within Upon Everything*.
- Write some sentences incorporating the examples of Cockney rhyming slang. Perhaps you could make up some rhyming slang of your own.

CONTAMINATION.

" I say, Jim, jist look if a smut hain't bin and settled on my Nose."

" Yes! A nasty little speck o' white plaster from that 'ere Scaffolding."

" Ugh! Jist blow it horf, will yer ?"

Punch, 2 May 1863

Examples of Cockney rhyming slang:

apples and pears (stairs)

Barnet fair (hair)

butcher's hook (look)

loaf of bread (head)

pen and ink (stink)

half-inch (pinch – steal)

Rosy Lee (tea)

tea leaf (thief)

dicky bird (word)

donkey's ears (years)

china plate (mate)

plates of meat (feet)

viii. Cockney Flunkey. — (*Country Footman meekly inquires of London Footman*)—" Pray, sir, what do you think of our town ? A nice place, ain't it ?" *London Footman (condescendingly).* " Vell, Joseph, I likes your town well enough. It's clean : your streets are hairy : and you have lots of rewins. But I don't like your champagne, it's all gewsberry !"

ix. Cockney Cabby (*with politeness*). — " Beg pardon, sir ; please don't smoke in the keb, sir ; ladies do complain o' the 'bacca uncommon. Better let me smoke it for yer outside, sir !"

x. Military Cockney. — *Lieutenant Blazer (of the Plungers).* — " Gwood gwacious ! Here's a howible go ! The infantwy's going to gwow a moustache !" *Cornet Huffey (whose face is whiskerless).* " Yaw don't mean that ! Wall ! there's only one alternative for us. WE must shave !"

xi. Juvenile Low Cockney.—"Jack ; Whereabouts i Amstid-am ?" *Jack.* " Well, I can't say exackerley, but I know it's somewhere near 'Ampstid-'eath !"

xii. Cockney Domestic. — *Servant girl.* — " Well, mam — Heverythink considered, I'm afraid you won't suit me. I've always bin brought up genteel: and I couldn't go nowheres where there ain't no footman kep'."

xiv. Cockney Waiter.—" 'Am, sir ? Yessir ? Don't take anything with your 'am, do you, sir ?" *Gentleman.* " Yes, I do ; I take the letter H !"

xv. Cockney Hairdresser.—" They say, sir, the cholera is in the Hair, sir !" *Gent (very uneasy).* " Indeed ! Ahem ! Then I hope you're very particular about the brushes you use." *Hairdresser.* " Oh, I see you don't hunderstand me, sir ; I don't mean the 'air of the 'ed, but the hair hof the hatmosphere ?"

xvi. Cockney Sweep (*seated upon a donkey*). — " Fitch us out another penn'orth o' strawberry hice, with a doll 'p o' lemon water in it."

xvii. Feminine Cockney (*by the seaside.*).—"Oh, Harriet, dear, put on your hat and let us thee the stheamboat come in. The thea is tho rough !—and the people will be *tho* abthurdly thick !"

xiii. Another.—*Lady.* " Wish to leave ! why, I thought, Thompson, you were very comfortable with me !" *Thompson (who is extremely refined).* " Ho yes, mum ! I don't find no fault with you, mum—nor yet with master— but the truth *his*, mum—the *hother* servants is so orrid vulgar and hignorant, and speaks so hungrammatical, that I reely cannot live in the same 'ouse with 'em—and I should like to go this day month, if so be has it won't illconvenience you !"

Enquire Within Upon Everything

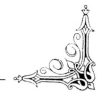

Victorian problems

Stimulus material

- Extract from Answers to Correspondents pages: *The Girls' Own Paper*, Volume 9, 1887–8.

Background

Each issue of *The Girl's Own Paper* contained answers to correspondents. These were responses to written questions submitted to the editorial team. However, the original questions were never published, leaving the reader to wonder about their content. The answers attempted to give advice on a wide range of subjects. The rules of correspondence were that writers should use initials or pseudonyms rather than their real names to ensure that their true identity would not be revealed to other readers.

Suggested activity

- Read the stimulus material. Use some of the answers and your imagination to write the 'original' questions or letters that prompted them.

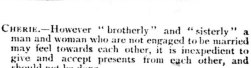

THE GIRL'S OWN PAPER

DISTRESSED MOTHER.—First speak to the boy kindly, but very firmly, and warn him that, should he despise kind and gentle commands, you will, with much pain and regret, have to resort to measures that will enforce obedience, by application to his schoolmaster. If he prove your master in this thing, the boy will become so in matters still graver. You do not name his age. You will have to report the case to his schoolmaster, and leave him to incur punishment at school—slight at first, and severe afterwards, till he be conquered.

FLOTOE.—Your friend should have consulted a doctor, or some sensible person, before venturing to give you such very bad advice as "to drink vinegar to make you thin"! Do you never read our Answers to Correspondents? If you did, you would have seen our warnings given to scores of girls who asked the same question. Do you wish to become dropsical, and exchange good flesh for watery puffings and bloating?

MYRTLE.—We are sorry for your nose. To wear a cracked chilblain on the end must be trying; but we do not like to prescribe for that member what we should for the hands. Keep yourself warm, and beware of approaching the fire when you come in from walking in the cold air. Perhaps you might effect a cure by holding your nose in a cup of very hot water for five minutes; and then, while smoking, in cold water for a minute, and dry with a soft handkerchief. Apply vaseline afterwards.

AN ANXIOUS WIFE.—We truly sympathise with you in having so timid a "worser half." His is indeed a bad case if obliged to "look under all the chairs and tables, as well as into the cupboards at night; and even then is so afraid to go up to bed!" Why he should carry this craze of peeping into unseen nooks and corners so far as to looking inside his envelopes several times before closing them, we could not explain, as burglars could scarcely avail themselves of such a hiding-place, and we think, under such circumstances, you should obtain medical advice.

A DESPAIRING ONE.—We are very sorry to hear you have failed to pass your examination, and can only advise you to try again. We do not at all agree with your idea "that the only thing that can be done for you is to run away to London and try to get on the stage," nor do we see how that would help you. We are sorry to hear they are unkind to you at home in consequence of your failure, and we can only advise you to bear everything with patience and humility; and thus to learn valuable lessons of self-restraint and sweet temper which may be a blessing to you all through your life.

HYGIENE.—Try the effect of taking a tepid bath, quickly accomplished at night, if more convenient than in the morning. It would probably tend, however, towards making you wakeful. A certain amount of washing for cleanliness is essential at night, as well as in the morning; but complete immersion, we think, would drive away all inclination to sleep.

CHERIE.—However "brotherly" and "sisterly" a man and woman who are not engaged to be married may feel towards each other, it is inexpedient to give and accept presents from each other, and should not be done.

"ONE (VERY JUSTLY) PUNISHED."—Your parents were right in being very angry with you for playing such a trick on your little sister. She did not know what she had to expect, as she had never seen the "ghost" which you older children had been entertained with at the party, and might have been frightened into fits and made an idiot for life! You would not have hidden in the cupboard when your father came, unless you had been quite aware that you had been doing wrong.

JENNIE.—To prevent lamps from smoking, the wick should be soaked in strong vinegar, and dried well before being used. The wick should also be very carefully cut, and kept perfectly straight.

LEIGH.—We have given an article on the subject of the tricycle for ladies some time ago, and in our monthly dress article you will find a suitable dress given, with directions for making it. We think the tricycle affords a capital means of taking exercise and gaining both amusement and change of air.

INA.—A girl from thirteen to fifteen should go to bed at nine o'clock, get up at seven, and breakfast at eight. But there is no hard and fast rule, as they should go to bed when sent by their mother, or person in whose charge they are placed. There can be no appeal against their wishes.

STABLE BOY.—We do not see that it is any affair of yours, or of ours either, whether a lady wear a wig or not, and whether she has lost her hair through illness; there is no need for making any excuses about it. Do not make personal remarks about anyone, and avoid puerile gossip. We think that smoking is a horrible practice for women.

CRITIC AND GOVERNESS (?).—This young person sends us a note containing ten ill-spelt words, and yet has the audacity to inquire "what celery she should get as a nursery governess." We should prefer paying to keep her out of the house, judging her by her style of writing and spelling and the impertinence of her letter.

GREY WAGTAIL.—You are very wise in your decision to take a situation as domestic servant; but you will need proper training for any situation you may select. As an under nurse you could learn of the upper one, and gain experience, so as to rise in time. As a lady's maid you should be a good needlewoman, learn hairdressing, millinery, and dressmaking; and to fit yourself for other positions you might try to get into the Industrial and Training School for Girls, 3, Church Street, Kensington, where girls are received between the ages of twelve and sixteen, to be trained for domestic service. Apply to the hon. lady secretary, 19, Southwell Gardens, South Kensington, London. There is also the Clapham Servants' Training Institution, 63, High Street, Clapham, London. Write to hon. sec., Holywood, Clapham Common.

Code crackers

Stimulus material
- Encypted advertisements from *The Times*, 1853.
- Advice about encryption from *Enquire Within Upon Everything*, 1884.

Background
Men and women wishing to declare their love for each other sometimes placed secret advertisements called cryptograms on the front page of *The Times*. It became a national pastime to try to crack the secret codes used to place these advertisements. Some years later, *Enquire Within Upon Everything* explained how to write and decipher messages. However, encoding and deciphering was time-consuming and prone to errors. Even the example in *Enquire Within Upon Everything* contains some mistakes!

Suggested activities
- Use the code from *Enquire Within Upon Everything* to translate these words:

  82xx* 3a 5* 12

- Write a short message using the code provided in *Enquire Within Upon Everything*. See if a partner can translate it.
- Use the translation key provided by *Enquire Within Upon Everything* to translate the speech from *Hamlet*. This is not easy since the example contains some mistakes! (Answer at bottom of page.)

Extension activity
- Aim to crack the codes in *The Times* article. The authors have not succeeded in doing so!

Ham. Angels and ministers of grace defend us!
Be thou a spirit of health or goblin damn'd.

TO M. M. M.——ALL WELL.

NODNOL.—LETTERS await you at the post office of the place whence your letter of the 31st July was addressed.

Nb Wvzivhg Z. Lfi ozhg xbksvi szh yvvm ivzw hl mfhg xsxmtvrg. Rgdzh rmgsv Grmvh zufigmrtsg ztl. Rnfhg dirgv gilblf zmwhvmw blf zmvd xibkgltinks. Ovgnv pmkd dsviv Rxxm dirgv klhgv Irhgzmgv, dsviv blfxzrm irwr lfg zohnv mzw tvgrg—

S lmpi F. npi. C qgnl. F. mhqo opnl qmnp lph. O qkin lgi F. npi C qgnl F. hkom ikpq kbq pil opki ikpq oh ongl qolg B. pmmh F. mkhg 8: F. hkom C klnh F. oinl B q_l O nkh F. inqg nmkq C holm. F. hmig C. hgo. F npi npkl iq hlom hqi pil. C qgnl F. nmkq ophq lqoi plg C kgql F. mlgi 2nd einq lqkh mg omnl plg C qkip 8. F. qmkg C. ngil F. oghm npkl ikmn npkl ngl mik logk npkl qlgo. C qlin qkin B. nkq C lgi F. pil. C hgo. F oghm hipo lgkh. qik ong hnio ikpn.—T. B.C.

CRYPTOGRAPH.—W. M.——Le beau temps Viendra would further oblige one whom he has already greatly obliged by FORWARDING his ADDRESS to the same direction as before.

The Times, 1 September 1853

FLO. 1821 82374 29 30 84541. 185270 924 184 182 82460. 84314 8842 31 8599420 31 8355 7239241 8218. 726 85400 021.

The Times, 21 September 1853

Where one letter is always made to stand for another, the secret of a cryptograph is soon discovered, but when, as in the following example, the same letter does not invariably correspond to the letter for which it is a substitute, the difficulty of deciphering the cryptograph is manifestly increased :—

Ohs ya h sych, oayarsa rr loucys syms
Osrh srore rrhmu h smsmsmah emshyr sums.

The translation of this can be made only by the possessor of the key.

a b c d e f g h i j k l m n o p q r s
h u s h m o n e y b y c h a r l e s h
t u v w x y z
r o s s e s q

"Hush Money, by Charles H. Ross, Esq."—twenty-six letters which, when applied to the cryptograph, will give a couplet from Parnell's "Hermit":—

"Far in a wild, unknown to public view, From youth to age a reverend hermit grew."

The employment of figures and signs for letters is the most usual form of the cryptograph. From the following jumble we get a portion of Hamlet's address to the Ghost :—

9 a 6 2 × ‡ 9 a 1 ‖ 3 a 3 ‡ 2 † ‡ * 7 6 †
9 5 2 1 2 7 2 a 1 ; ‡
4 2 8 * ; ‡ (3 † 3 , * 7 8 2 0 × , 1 * †
6 * 4 × 3 a 1 9 ‖ a 2 1

With the key—

a b c d e f g h i j k l m n o p q r s
9 4 5 1 2 7 6 8 3 + — × ‖ a * ( ) † ;
t u v w x y z
, ; : . o § ÷

it is easy to write and not very hard to read the entire speech. The whole theory of the cryptogram is that each correspondent possesses the key to the secret. To confound an outside inquirer the key is often varied. A good plan is to take a line from any ordinary book and substitute the first twenty-six of its letters for those of the alphabet. In your next cryptogram you take the letters from another page or another book. It is not necessary to give an example. Enough will be seen from what we have written to instruct an intelligent inquirer.

From *Enquire Within Upon Everything*

Amazing cures (1)

Stimulus material

- Advertisement for Du Barry's Ravalenta Arabica Food.
- Advertisement for Galvanic chain bands etc.
- Advertisement for the Carbolic Smoke Ball.
- Advertisement for Chlorodyne.

Background

Since there was no National Health Service in Victorian times, people had to pay for medical treatment. Advertisements appeared in the press for pills and gadgets that would make a visit to the doctor unnecessary.

The invisible forces of magnetism and electricity were often claimed to have healing powers. Some gadgets such as electro-magnetic machines, designed to produce electric shocks, were supposed to have a beneficial effect on rheumatism as well as headaches and toothache!

Galvanic chains carried letters of testimony from satisfied customers suggesting a much wider range of cures and improvements in health without pain.

Du Berry's Ravalenta Arabica Food was advertised as an alternative to taking pills. It was claimed to have cured 72,000 illnesses that had resisted all medical treatment.

Other manufacturers took a different approach. Their advertisements claimed that prevention was better than cure. Magnetic combs were sold to people wishing to prevent baldness, while the Carbolic Smoke Ball was meant to keep the user free from many common illnesses. The advertisement for the Carbolic Smoke Ball confidently offered £100 to anyone who used the product for two weeks and subsequently caught influenza. Unfortunately for the manufacturers, Lucy Carlill did just that. At first the company refused to pay, but she took them to court and won.

Suggested activities

- Write your own letter of testimony or complaint about a 'health-giving' product.
- Design your own advertisement for a similar product.

Amazing cures (2)

Stimulus material

- Extract from *Nicholas Nickleby* by Charles Dickens.

Background

The eccentric and somewhat confused Mrs Nickleby attempts to recall using a self-help remedy.

Suggested activities

- Make up your own self-help cures for a range of common complaints (not life-threatening ones).
- Write diary extracts for people who have tried these cures.

I had a cold once," said Mrs. Nickleby, "I think it was in the year eighteen hundred and seventeen; let me see, four and five are nine, and—yes eighteen hundred and seventeen, that I thought I never should get rid of; actually and seriously, that I thought I never should get rid of. I was only cured at last by a remedy that I don't know whether you ever happened to hear of, Mr. Pluck. You have a gallon of water as hot as you can possibly bear it, with a pound of salt and sixpen'orth of the finest bran, and sit with your head in it for twenty minutes every night just before going to bed; at least, I don't mean your head —your feet. It's a most extraordinary cure—a most extraordinary

cure. I used it for the first time, I recollect, the day after Christmas day, and by the middle of April following the cold was gone. It seems quite a miracle when you come to think of it, for I had it ever since the beginning of September."

Extract from *Nicholas Nickleby* by Charles Dickens

Somnambulism
(sleep-walking)

Stimulus material

- The Curious Case of Somnambulism: *News of the World*, 1 October 1843.
- Answers to Correspondents: *The Girl's Own Paper*, 14 July 1888.

Background

Somnambulism (sleep-walking) affects many children and some adults. In the 'Curious Case' reported in the *News of the World* in 1843, the mistress of a house awakes to find one of her servants doing her chores in her sleep!

The Girl's Own Paper (14 July 1888) gives advice on dealing with the problem.

Suggested activities

- Read the article and advice about somnambulism. Imagine awaking from a good sleep to find that you have just completed your homework or household chores. However, perhaps there are other activities that you would rather be awake for, a visit to a theme park or eating a favourite meal for example.
- Make a list under the following headings:

Five Things to Avoid While Asleep!
Five Things to Do While Asleep!

CURIOUS CASE OF SOMNAMBULISM. — A few days ago the mistress of a respectable house in the Vauxhall-road was disturbed during the night by the scratching and noise made at her bed-room door on the second floor by a favourite dog, whose general place of repose was in the kitchen. The mistress at first imagined that the dog made the noise merely to get into the room, and rose from her bed to admit him, but on lying down again the dog jumped upon the bed, and by pulling at her sleeve and using every means available to a dumb animal, endeavoured to show that he wanted her to follow him. On pushing the dog down from the bed, she found he was wet all over, and being fearful of some accident having happened below she arose from her bed and descended the stairs with the faithful animal, and, after some difficulty, succeeded in obtaining a light in the kitchen. The first place the mistress examined was her servant's bed, to ascertain from her if she had heard any noise, or could account for the conduct of the dog, when, to her astonishment, she found the bed empty. Naturally alarmed at the absence of the servant, she listened for some time in a state of great suspense, fearing that some parties might have entered the house, and at last heard a noise in the back kitchen, as of some person cleaning knives or forks, and on going in that direction to her great surprise witnessed her servant standing in her night clothes, and without shoes or stockings cleaning forks, with her eyes shut, and evidently in deep sleep. The mistress, after in some degree recovering from her surprise, passed the candle two or three times across the servant's face, but the girl continued her work with her eyes still shut, unconscious of any other person being present ; and, after rubbing the fork in her hand on the board, held it up to her shut eyes, as if examining that it was sufficiently polished, then took the leather to wipe the dust off, and passed it as carefully and correctly between every prong as if she had been wide awake. The mistress on examining what had been done, in a state of somnambulism, found by a tub of water on the floor that she had washed the dog, her usual task, and had cleaned a dozen of knives and seven forks, and was proceeding with cleaning the others, when the unusual motions of the dog attracted his mistress to the spot were the servant was at work. The mistress removed the uncleaned forks out of the reach of the servant, and taking hold of the sleeve of her night gown, gently moved her towards her bed, but whether from an internal sense of the work she was engaged in not being finished, or the action of the light of the candle on her eyelids, she awoke on the floor, but was quite unconscious of what had taken place. The mistress put the girl to bed, concealing from her what had been done, and at an after period of the night visited her bed, but it did not appear that she had again got up in her sleep.

News of the World, 1 October 1843

SHADRACH.—Sleepwalkers should never be wakened while out of bed ; they should be led gently back, and then wakened and scolded for having got up. If this do not prove effectual in breaking the habit, they should be tied to the bed, and candle and matches placed beyond their reach. Also, there should be no exciting conversation nor exciting book read before going to bed.

The Girl's Own Paper:
Answers to Correspondents,
16 July 1888

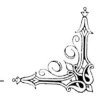

Defying death

Stimulus material

- Article reporting Blondin's first show at the Crystal Palace: from *The Times*, 3 June 1861.
- Picture of Blondin.
- List of Blondin merchandise.

Background

World-famous tightrope walker Blondin came to London having gained his fame performing on a rope suspended above the rapids close to Niagara Falls. To encourage spectators, he developed ever more daring routines. Crowds flocking to watch his shows were offered a range of souvenir merchandise (see list).

Suggested activities

- Imagine that you are a daring Victorian performer. What would you call yourself? What would you do to attract the crowds? Where would you perform?
- Write a newspaper report of your performance. You may wish to use some phrases taken from the 1861 *Times* report to help you.
- Look at the list of Blondin merchandise. What merchandise would you make available to the crowds coming to watch you? Draw and label some designs.
- Make a poster to advertise your next show or Blondin's next show.

He wore the dress of an Indian chief, the same in which he performed before the Prince of Wales, and which is formed entirely of those most beautiful specimens of Indian bondwork which are offered to visitors at the Falls. Without chalking either his feet or the rope, or any of those hesitating preliminaries in which minor artistes so indulge to impress the public with the perils of their vocation, he came out at once upon the rope, standing on each leg alternately, motionless as a statue. The "sag" or droop of the cable from a straight line is 12 feet; at Niagara it was nearly 40, and was there almost a source of danger. On Saturday he quite disregarded this slight incline, and, after showing how perfectly at home he was by balancing his pole on the rope and standing on his head in the centre of it, he dropped at once flat on his back, turned a summersault backwards, caught up his pole, and ran as swiftly almost as a man would run on the ground across the rope to the other side of the building. He then walked backwards, again stood on his head, again lay on his back, and ran about with a freedom of motion and certainty of step that to the spectators was utterly incomprehensible. There was no balancing, no movement of the pole from side to side, every feat on this inch-and-a-half rope, 180 feet from the ground, was done with the same certainty and the same apparent ease as if he was performing on the floor so far beneath. He next had his eyes firmly bandaged, and over his head was placed a new sack with holes in the side for his arms. Thus hampered, he again ventured out upon the cord, though this time feigning uncertainty and doubt, with cautious trembling footsteps that raised the spectators' fear and anxiety to the very utmost. Thrice he pretended to miss the rope, and reeled and staggered on it in a way that made every one's blood run cold. Then, instantly throwing off his hesitation, he ran quickly along the rope, stood on his head, lay on his back, turned a summersault backwards, and all this still blindfold and enveloped in his canvass bag.

The Times, 3 June 1861

Blondin merchandise:

Blondin soup
Blondin lemonade
Blondin stringed puppets
Blondin pop-up book

Further death-defying challenges

Stimulus material
- List of Blondin's stunts.
- Extract from the *McKean Citizen* making fun of Blondin.

Background
Blondin left the Niagara Falls area because the crowds began to get smaller. Some journalists had begun to get bored at his performances because there seemed little chance that he would have an accident. To ease the boredom, a few began to make fun of him by making up ludicrous challenges and reports.

Suggested activities
- Read the list of Blondin's death-defying stunts on the high wire above the Niagara rapids. Did you notice the last one?
- Imagine that you were the person carried on Blondin's back. Write a diary entry to describe what happened. Record what Blondin said to you, what you saw when you looked down, the reaction of the crowd, how you felt when Blondin told you that he needed a rest half-way across, the most terrifying moment, your feelings when you were close to the other side.
- Write an eye-witness report from a spectator in the crowd.
- Write a new challenge for Blondin. This could be a serious challenge or a humorous one in the style of the article in the *McKean Citizen*.

A single telegraph wire shall be extended from the American to the Canadian shore, without a single guy, directly over the cataract at Niagara Falls. The 'local' [correspondent] of this paper, wearing cowhide boots and dressed in the costume of a female Dutch cook, will proceed to the middle of the wire, with a common clay pipe as a balancing pole, driving before him a hog and a cow, and carrying on his back a cooking-stove, a coop of chickens, a bed and bedding, a keg of lager beer, a bather's chair, and various cooking utensils. He will then unload himself and immediately go to bed. After a snooze of fifteen minutes he will rise, dress himself, take a glass of beer, milk the cow, kill the hog and dress it, cook fresh pork for breakfast, after which he will eat a wolf's meal. He will then throw one hundred and thirty summersaults [*sic*], sucking an egg while in the air at each evolution, alighting the last time on the top of the cow's horn, and while in this position will take the chicken coop, and after having taken the chickens out one at a time and wrung their necks consecutively, will balance the cooking-stove on his right hand thumb, balance the bedstead on his left thumb at the same time finishing the beer and making a Dutch speech to the admiring crowds on either shore . . . The foreman of this paper will then come out on the wire, blindfolded and shackled, walking on his hands. There will then be a representation of Heenan and Morrissey's prize-fight, in which the 'local' and foreman will exchange sundry knocks and kicks and black eyes. The whole to conclude with a representation of some of the loving scenes in Romeo and Juliet.

Extract from *McKean Citizen*, September 1859

A List of Blondin's Stunts on the High Wire:

Lie down, stand on one foot, open a bottle of wine, walk backwards, push a wheelbarrow, hang from the rope by hands, feet and one ankle, cross with ankles in chains, perform a backwards somersault, lie on the rope and move along it like a swimmer, walk across on stilts, in a monkey suit, playing a drum, carry a cooking stove complete with bellows, sit down in the middle, cook an omelette, carry a person across on his back.

Victorian celebrity fact file

Stimulus material
- Pictures of Victorian performers Leotard and Madame Zazal.
- Lyrics from 'The Daring Young Man on the Flying Trapeze' (music hall song sung by Gorge Leybourne, 1868).

Background

Large crowds gathered to watch performances of daring and courage. Some performers became celebrities.

Leotard was famous for his routines on the flying trapeze. Today, dancers and performers wear 'leotards' named after him.

Madame Zazal became famous as 'The Human Cannon Ball'.

Suggested activities

Try to find out about these, or other famous performers. You could compile a fact file.

Support

Performer's name: _____

Date born: _____

Place of birth: _____

Became famous by: _____

Performed at (names of places): _____

Further information: _____

Extension activities
- Choose one of these performers and write a more detailed biography.
- Use the information you have collected to write an imaginary interview with one of the performers for a magazine. You could make this a Victorian magazine or a modern one which has discovered the secret of time travel. You could mix factual answers with made-up ones to make an interesting article. You could arrange your question and answers in chronological order so that they tell the life story of your chosen performer. Open-ended questions beginning with Who . . . ?, What . . . ?, When . . . ?, Where . . . ?, Why . . . ? and How . . . ? will make your interview interesting.

'The Daring Young Man On the Flying Trapeze'

He'd fly through the air with the greatest of ease,
A daring young man on the flying trapeze,
His movements were graceful,
All the girls he could please,
And my love he has purloined away.

(Music hall song sung by
George Leybourne, 1868)

One trick too many

Stimulus material
· The Death of Madam Genieve (*Punch*, 1863).

Background
Madame Genieve became famous as the 'Female Blondin'. Tragically, she died at Aston Park, Birmingham when her tightrope snapped as she crossed it blindfolded. Many people began to criticise such performances and some called for them to be banned altogether. Even Queen Victoria wrote to the Mayor of Birmingham to complain. Despite, or perhaps because of a number of similar accidents, people continued to flock to daring performances.

Suggested activities
· Make a list of modern spectator events that have an element of risk, for example Formula One, downhill skiing. With your partner, discuss whether you think these events should be allowed.

· Write a persuasive letter to a newspaper explaining whether you think that life-threatening performances should be allowed. (You may write about your own views on modern events, or you may wish to set it in the past and write from the point of view of someone who shares Queen Victoria's views or a Victorian who enjoys performances involving risk.)

Support
You could start your letter like this:

Dear

Many people enjoy watching dangerous events such as

_____ and _____ .

I believe that they should/not be allowed to continue to do so. I have several reasons for this point of view.

First, . . .

Second, . . .

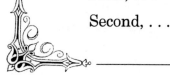

DEATH ON THE ROPE.

LATEST FROM PRU

Half a score more newspa
suppressed by the Police for th
reasons which we here subjoin

For saying that King Will
head last Wednesday, but the
suppose that there was nothing

For saying that in Englanc
talk politics without being beh

For criticising the appearan
Dolles his hat, and repeating
some one had been somewher
he wore a white one.

For quoting the statement in
English history, that King
First walked and talked hal
his head was cut off.

For using the word "pig
leading article about the K
mey, it being obvious that I
was the personage referred to

For prophesying that the
when Prussia will no longe
roughly free press.

For saying that a Policen
last week in London in the
Cook: this statement being
the view to bring discredit
constables in general, and t
in particular.

For stating as a fact in N
that a Cat may look at a Ku
he be a Prussian one.

Architectura

The process of restorat
proved a benefit to other wor
of the Mediæval church bu
glad to hear that within the
very good umbrella has been

Advice Gratis.—An
writes to know what is the
her little son John? We sho

KILLING NO MURDER!
THE DANCE OF DEATH IN REALITY.
NOVELTY, TERRIFIC AND THRILLING!

The Committee of the Ancient Order of Slaughterers beg to announce
to the Nobility, Gentry and Mining Public in general, that their Annual
Fête will take place on Monday next, on which occasion an entertainment of unparalleled sensational interest will be produced for this day
only.

An infant ten months old will be discharged from

A CATAPULT
(Registered)

OVER A REGIMENT OF SOLDIERS WITH FIXED BAYONETS!

The Committee feeling a deeply-rooted aversion to all performances
of a brutalising nature, and anxious to give confidence to the most
nervous spectator, have at an enormous expense provided an

AIR MATTRESS,

Which will be laid down within range of the projectile.

After which Dancing to Cripples' Band, the whole to conclude with

A Grand Display of Fireworks.

Introducing new and beautiful devices, representing

A SKELETON!

In the last stage of intoxication, illuminated by blue candles and ani-
mated by

LAUGHING GAS!!

N.B. No money—under any circumstances—returned.

NOISY NEWS-CRIERS.

Literature is a good thing, and so is exercise
sometimes when combined they are productive of a
the calling of cheap newspapers by loud-voiced little I
in London most undoubtedly become. No sooner does
into a train of quiet thought than the '*Apenny O'born*
into his ears; and this in a few moments is follow
Newgate News, or the *Farthing Strand Gazette.*

Nearly every parish has its local "organ" for expres
and these organs are almost as great a nuisance as the
their names are bawled and shrieked and screamed and
the streets in a manner quite distracting to men of q
who are not deaf. On a Sunday morning, too, when
row one sighs to be at peace, some of the cheap weekly
cried; and the bellowing of their names is as much a
as that of "Chayny owringe," or "Fine fresh Hob-o-o
one's ears are tortured later in the day.

Whether the Police have power to stop these cri
which Sir Richard Mayne may kindly look to: but
papers are a new invention, it is doubtful if old Act
extend to them. *Mr. Punch* would therefore ask th
Relief of Quiet People like himself should be brought i
ment without the least delay; and he trusts that in t
permission will be granted him, and all tormented pers
risk of finding themselves fined for an assault, to wollo
kick, thrash, and summarily punish any penny-paper-c
they can catch.

Thoughtful Editing.

The new number of the *Quarterly* seems arranged
the season. The prominent articles are, the Glacial Th
of Rome, and Spiritualism. Come, Ice, Wafer, and Lic
hints in this weather.

Punch, 1 August 1863

Object lessons

Stimulus material

- List of titles for object lessons from Victorian school log book.
- Extract from Inspector's Report.

Background

Instead of science, children were taught about the world through 'object lessons'. The teacher would show the children an object or a picture and tell them about it. The children were often required to repeat the information given. Since there was no television in those days, and many children stayed very close to home, this was a way of extending their general knowledge.

Suggested activities

Imagine that you are a Victorian teacher. Choose a subject from the lists of object lessons. Prepare a short talk to give to the rest of the class. Your talk will be more memorable if you show something to the pupils in your class. (No lions, tigers, eagles, monkeys, reindeer or whales please!)

April 1892 List of Object Lessons for Infants Class
Spider, Silkworm, Tiger, Lion, Whale, Reindeer
Eagle, Herring, Monkey, Owl, Bee, Brown Bear
Pear, Rice, Coffee, Orange, Lead, Gold, Iron
Coins, Glue, Bakers shop, Butchers shop
Writing a letter, Farmyard, Kitchen articles
Sun, Clouds, Night and day, Wind.

page 365, April 1892

List of Object Lessons for Infants Class
Spider, silkworm, tiger, lion, whale, reindeer, eagle, herring, monkey, owl, bee, brown bear, pear, rice, coffee, orange, lead, gold, iron, coins, glue, baker's shop, writing a letter, farmyard, kitchen articles, sun, clouds, night and day, wind.

page 335, 1889

Object Lessons and Varied Occupations
Animal: Lion, cow, horse, eagle, ostrich, peacocke, monkey, mouse.
Vegetable: Buttercup, fir tree, orange, potato, dandelion, holly.
Mineral: Silver, lead, iron, slate.
Trades: Fisherman, butcher.
Natural Phenomena: A windy day, the sun, frost water, rainbow.
Miscellaneous: Hand, eye, lead pencil, chair, letter.
Kindergarten.: Paper plaiting, embroidery, drawing, ball making, bead threading.

Object Lessons and Varied Occupations
Animal: Lion, cow, horse, eagle, ostrich, peacock, monkey, mouse.
Vegetable: Buttercups, fir tree, orange, potato, dandelion, holly.
Mineral: Silver, lead, iron, slate
Trades: Fisherman, butcher
Natural Phenomena: A windy day, the sun, frost water, rainbow.
Miscellaneous: Hand, eye, lead pencil, chair, letter.

page 440, 1899–1900

Standard III Object Lessons.
A balloon, steam engine, diving bell, siphon and pump, porosity, glass, cocoa, nut, plums and berries, oats, fur, starch, carbon, coffee, stems of trees, sugar, roots of plants, leaves of plants, oil, mustard, food of plants, alum, evergreen trees, alcohol, a piece of granite, oak tree, linen, preservation of foods, India rubber,

Stand. III. A Balloon, Steam Engine, Diving Bell, Siphon & Pump
Porosity, Glass, Cocoa Nut, Plums & Berries, Oats,
Fur, Starch, Carbon, [illegible], Stems of trees, Sugar,
Roots of Plants, Leaves of Plants, Oil, Mustard,
Food of Plants, Alum, Berries, Evergreen Trees,
Alcohol, A Piece of Granite, Oak tree, Linen,
Preservation of Food, India rubber,

Infants' Class. The Infants are in excellent order and have been very carefully and on the whole very successfully taught. More attention must be given to Physical Exercises and care must be taken that the Object Lessons are all well thought out and properly illustrated
E. Wells is continued under Article 68. of the Code
The School Staff consists of Miss

Misbehaving pupils

Stimulus material

- Extacts from school log book.

Background

The school master or mistress was required to record a daily diary of events at school. These included records of pupil misbehaviour.

Suggested activities

- In small groups, act out chosen scenes described in the log book.
- In your groups, decide: What the teacher said; What questions did he or she ask?; How did the pupils respond?
- 'Freeze frame' the start and the end of each short scene. Take turns in being the teacher for each scene.

Boys had no play this afternoon in consequence of a window having been cracked in Sunday School.

Gave a caution to 5 boys who brought with them potash, brimstone and powder and since then nothing of the kind has been seen.

Several scholars punished today for being late twice or oftener during the week. There is now a great improvement in the attendance at 9 a.m. and 1.30 but there is still often late scholars, notwithstanding all are kept in at playtime and after school.

Neighbour complained of our scholars throwing stones.

The time for singing on Friday was mostly taken up by giving instruction to the school on these points:

Order in the lines.

Order outside the school when going home.

Cleanliness of slates.

Cautioned several boys against throwing stones.

Last, in inquiring into a disgraceful fight in Cross Street on Thursday evening.

Punished all the late scholars without notes.

The same again.

Fewer late scholars.

Punished two boys this week for lying.

Three or four boys have been punished for bad writing nearly every day this week.

Punished and warned scholars for leaving the school premises during the dinner hour to bathe.

Punished a boy for kicking a girl on leaving school last evening.

Cautioned several boys about throwing stones and punished three for fighting in the playground on Thursday afternoon.

Head teacher suffered from bad throat. Had to give orders through a boy.

From 11.30 to 12 departed from routine to speak to children on gallery about theft; a boy having brought a bagful of cigars from home and distributing amongst the boys. Sent for the boy's mother and found that he had been rather troublesome before in other things.

Spoke to the whole school about behaviour in consequence of two boys having gone under the gallery at playtime and remained under after having sent for them.

Made them stand away from the lesson and remain to do it after school.

Extracts from school log book, 1864–87

School Inspector's Report

Stimulus materials
- The expectations and assessment of pupil teachers.
- The names of some pupil teachers from a school record book.

Background
Pupil teachers were children who stayed on at school after the leaving age to learn to be teachers themselves. They were expected to help the teacher by teaching younger children, and they had to study and take exams.

Suggested activities
Look at the expectations of pupil teachers and some of the names of real pupil teachers during Victorian times. Imagine that you are a school inspector. Choose one of the pupil teacher's names, and write an imaginary report on one of them. You may use the following framework to help to structure your work if you wish.

_____ (name of pupil teacher) has a pleasant/gentle/harsh manner with the scholars. Her/his pronunciation is clear/indistinct/inaudible. S/he lacks energy/is energetic in delivering lessons.

During my observation, the scholars were mainly attentive/inattentive and active/lazy. The noise level was low/rather high excessively high/intolerable.

The lesson was well ordered/lacked order. Many of the children appear to understand their work/show a lack of understanding.

_____ (name of pupil teacher) was patient/impatient with the scholars who needed further help.

S/he made good use/little use/no use of drawings and illustrations to support this lesson.

In my professional opinion, this pupil teacher is making poor/reasonable/good/excellent progress.

Signed _____ (Inspector's name)

Date _____ 18 _____

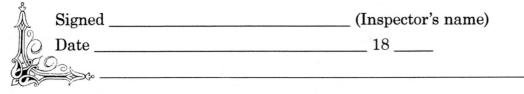

Reading.	Grammar.	Writing and Composition.	Arithmetic, Mechanics, Mensuration, Land Surveying, Levelling, and Algebra.	Geography.	Religious Knowledge. In Church of England Schools only, the Clergyman assisting in the Examination.	Religious Knowledge. In Schools not being Church of England Schools, nor coming under the Minute of 10th July 1847.*	Skill in Teaching. H. M.'s Inspector will pay particular attention to the Modulation of the Voice.	Vocal Music, and Drawing from Models.
To Read with fluency, ease, and expression. (1)	To point out the Parts of Speech in a simple sentence.	To write in a neat hand, with correct spelling, and punctuation, a simple prose narrative slowly read to them. (1)	To write from dictation Sums in the first four Rules of Arithmetic, Simple and Compound, and to work them correctly, and to know the Tables of Weights and Measures. (1)	To have an elementary knowledge of Geography. (1)	To repeat the Church Catechism and to show that they understand its meaning, and are acquainted with the outlines of Scripture History. (1)	Certificate from the Managers of the School that the Religious Knowledge of the Pupil Teacher or Stipendiary Monitor is satisfactory to them.	To teach a Junior Class to the satisfaction of the Inspector.	
Improved articulation and expression in Reading.	The construction of Sentences and Syntax.(2)	To write from memory the substance of a more difficult narrative. (3)	Practice (2), [Simple Proportion, and the first Rules of Mental Arithmetic].	The Geography of Great Britain and Palestine.	The Holy Scriptures and Catechism, with Illustrations by Passages from Holy Writ.	Same as above.	Ability to give a Class a Reading Lesson, and to examine it on the meaning of what has been read. (2) Ability [to drill a Class in marching and exercises, and] to conduct it through the movements required for preserving order.	Elements of Vocal Music taught when from Notes. Drawing from Models where there is proper Apparatus.
Improved articulation and expression in Reading.	Syntax [and Etymology]. (4)	Composition of a School Report [or the Minutes of a Lesson]. Stipendiary Monitors—to write from memory, with correct spelling and punctuation, the substance of a simple prose narrative read carefully to them two or three times.	Compound Proportion [Decimal Arithmetic], the higher Rules of Mental Arithmetic. (4)	The Geography of Great Britain, Europe (3), [the British Empire, and] Palestine.	The Holy Scriptures, Liturgy, and Catechism, more fully than in the preceding year.	Same as above.	Ability to examine a Class in Reading, in the rudiments of Grammar and Arithmetic, and during the examination to keep the Class attentive, in order, and in activity, without undue noise.	Elements of Vocal Music taught when from Notes. Drawing from Models where there is proper Apparatus.
Improved articulation and expression in Reading.	Syntax. Etymology (3), [and Prosody].	Composition of the Notes of a Lesson on a subject selected by the Inspector. (4)	[Elements of Mechanics] and Book-keeping.†	Geography of the British Empire (4) [and of the Four Quarters of the Globe]. Stipendiary Monitors—Geography of the outlines of the Four Quarters of the Globe	More fully in the Holy Scriptures, Liturgy, and Catechism.	Same as above.	Skill in managing and examining the Second Class in Grammar, Geography, and Mental Arithmetic.	Elements of Vocal Music taught when from Notes. Drawing from Models where there is proper Apparatus.

Pupil teachers: J. P. Hardman; Fred Chubb; John Sargent; E. Williams; John Butterworth; Ben Horrocks; J. Ainsworth; John Clegg; Mathew Ryley; J. Rawlinson; Emma Edwards; Janet Mitchell; Robina Russel; Eliza Hand; George Shufflebotham; M. Pickup

Victorian vandals

Stimulus material

- Extracts from school log book (Farnworth Wesleyan Chapel School).

Background

Victorian schools were often the target of vandalism.

Suggested activities

- Read the log book extracts. Imagine that you were an eye-witness to one of these incidents. Write a witness statement for the police or the local paper.

> *During the holidays some person or persons have got into the school probably through class room window. + have broken into my desk + one cupboard broken the locks + squandered the books paste all over the floor mischief not plunder seams to have been the motive as we have missed nothing save 20 penny pencils and a few pieces of india rubber —*

During the holidays some person or persons unknown have got into the school, probably through classroom window and have broken into my desk and the cupboard, broken the locks and squandered the books, pens etc all over the floor. Mischief, ~~not plunder seems to have been~~ the motive as we have missed nothing save 20 penny pencils and a few pieces of India rubber.

8 January 1877

> *Dec 3 Since Friday night the school has been entered, + locks have been forced three of which are broken. the stationery about 3 gross of copy Bks. Exercise Bks tc. were squandered on the floor & a bottle of red ink sprinkled over them penholders black, + slate pencils were broke + squandered similarly. An attempt had also been made to burn some of them. the door of the clock was also broken off.*

Since Friday night this school has been entered 4 locks have been forced three of which are broken: The stationery, about 3 gross of copy books, exercise books etc were squandered on the floor and a bottle of red ink sprinkled over them. Pen holders, blackboard slate pencils were broken and squandered similarly. An attempt had also been made to burn some of them. The door of the clock was broken off.

3 December 1877

What a nuisance

Stimulus material

- Extracts from the Police Clauses Acts (Source: *Mrs Beeton's Book of Household Management*).

Background

A range of public nuisances listed under the Police Clauses Act was punishable by a £2 fine. This was increased to £5 for some offences in the Metropolitan Police District. It was the duty of police constables to uphold the law.

Suggested activities

- Read the extracts from the Police Clauses Act.
- Make a list of annoying nuisances at your school and in your community.
- Write your own updated Police Clauses Act outlining some of the most annoying nuisances. Don't forget to list the penalties for breaking your anti-nuisance laws.

6. **Under the Police Clauses Acts.**

Within the Metropolitan Police district,[2] or in a borough or urban district[2] the following acts are punishable by a fine not exceeding £2.

Beating or shaking in the street a carpet, rug or mat, except door mats before 8 in the morning; leaving open any vault, or cellar, or underground room without sufficient fence, or leaving an open area or pit without a sufficient light at night;

Also the following acts which are calculated to injure or annoy others; causing any vehicle to stand in the street longer than is necessary for loading or unloading; driving, or allowing to stand, on any footway, any vehicle or animal; wantonly disturbing a householder by ringing or knocking without lawful excuse; wilfully and unlawfully extinguishing any lamp in a street; furiously riding or driving any horse or carriage[1] or furiously driving cattle; or within the Metropolitan Police district riding or driving so as to endanger the safety of any person; discharging firearms or throwing any missile to the danger of any person; making a bonfire or discharging fireworks in the street; flying a kite; or, in the Metropolitan Police district, playing any game to the annoyance of the inhabitants or persons in the street; making or using a slide in any thoroughfare; turning loose any horse or animal in the street; allowing to be at large any unmuzzled ferocious dog, or setting any dog or other animal to attack or put in fear any person or animal; suffering a dog to go at large, knowing, or having reasonable ground for believing, it to be in a rabid state, or to have been bitten by an animal reasonably supposed to be in that condition;[2]

.—Emptying any privy between 6 a.m. and 12 midnight; removing any nightsoil through a thoroughfare between 6 a.m. and 8 p.m., or removing it in a conveyance without a proper covering; keeping a pig-stye to the front of a street without a proper fence, or keeping pigs so near to the road as to be a common nuisance.

Within any town or district referred to above, *other than in the Metropolitan Police district,* the following acts are likewise punishable :—Placing any flower-pot or box or any heavy article in an upper window without sufficiently guarding against its being blown down; throwing anything from a house into the street, except snow thrown so as not to fall on any person passing by; ordering or permitting any servant to stand on the sill of any window, except in the basement, in order to do anything to the outside of the window or house.

Within the Metropolitan Police district the following acts also are punishable as offences :—Posting any bill or paper on any property without the consent of the owner; writing upon or defacing any building or fence; using any noisy instrument for the purpose of calling people together or of announcing any show or entertainment, or for the purpose of hawking, selling, distributing or collecting any article, or of obtaining money or alms; persisting in playing music in the street.

Any householder may, either personally or by his servant, or by a police-constable, require a street musician or singer to depart from the neighbourhood of his house, on account of the illness or the interruption of the ordinary occupations or pursuits of any inmate of the house, or for other reasonable or sufficient cause. On failure to comply with such requirement the offender may be arrested by a constable without warrant.

Street shouting.—" No person shall for the purpose of hawking, selling or advertising any newspaper call or shout in any street so as to cause an annoyance to the inhabitants of the neighbourhood." Penalty not exceeding £2. It is not necessary to prove that more than one inhabitant has been annoyed, if the act complained of was of a character likely to annoy the inhabitants generally.

Fruit rinds. Broken glass. etc.—" No person shall deposit in any street or public place to the danger of passenger, the rind of any orange, banana or other fruit or the leaves or refuse of any vegetable."—" No person shall throw, place or leave any bottle or any broken glass, nail or other sharp substance (not being road material), on or in any street or public place in such a postion as to be likely to cause injury to passengers or animals, or damage to property." Penalty not exceeding £2.

Window cleaning.—" Every person who in any street, to the obstruction, annoyance or danger of residents or passengers, orders or permits any person in his service to stand or kneel on the sill of any window for the purpose of cleaning or painting such window, or for any other purpose whatsoever, such sill being more than 6 feet in height from the level of the ground immediately below it, without support sufficient to prevent such person from falling, shall for every such offence forfeit and pay a sum not exceeding £5." And every person who actually stands or kneels on the sill of any window under such circumstances is liable to a penalty not exceeding £2.

Spitting.—" No person shall spit on the floor, side or wall of any public carriage, or of any public hall, public waiting-room, or place of public entertainment, whether admission thereto be obtained upon payment or not." Penalty not exceeding £2.

[1] In which term is included a bicycle.
[2] Within the Metropolitan Police District this offence is punishable by a penalty of £5, instead of £2 as elsewhere.

From *Mrs Beeton's Book of Household Management*

Booking an entertainment

Stimulus material

• Harrod's Stores Limited Catalogue: General Hire Department.

Background

A variety of travelling entertainers could be booked for parties, fetes and school entertainers through Harrod's Stores.

Suggested activities

• Read through the list of entertainments that could be booked through Harrod's.

• Imagine that you are a school master/mistress wishing to book an end-of-year entertainment. Which one would you choose?

• Compose a letter to be sent home with pupils. This should give details of the proposed entertainment, the date and the time. Don't forget to ask for a contribution to the cost (in pre-decimal money) and include a permission slip that could be filled in and returned to school.

GENERAL HIRE.

No. 22 DEPARTMENT—FIRST FLOOR.

MUSICAL SKETCHES.

£ s. d.

At the Piano, after the style of Corney Grain and Grossmith.

At intervals during the evening ... ... from £2

Repertoire of several Artistes on application.

Humorous, Musical, and Dramatic Recital by Lady and Gentleman, suitable for Drawing-room or Public Hall, very refined and amusing ... from £7 7 0

PALMISTRY.

The Eastern Palmist, Signor Rupert, the Eminent Character Delineator, for At Homes, Evening Parties, &c. Parents and Guardians should consult this Gentleman before deciding on the occupation of the children under their charge. The whole evening ... ... from 3 3 0

Also several Lady Palmists.

FORTUNE TELLER.

Lady Fortune Teller, in Gipsy Costume, 2 hours ... from 2 2 0

HAND-BELL RINGERS AND GLEE SINGERS.

The Royal Criterion Hand-bell Ringers and Glee Singers, 13 times honoured with Royal Patronage and Command, and have had the honour of playing to Her Majesty the Queen, the Prince of Wales, and other Members of the Royal Family and Nobility. Conductor, Mr. Harry Tipper, from 5 5 0

Hand-bell Solos with Pianoforte Accompaniment. A first-class Entertainment for Concerts, At Homes, &c. Every one says it is a charming performance ... ... from 3 18 0

Harry Tipper's Glee Party can be engaged separately ... from 5 5 0

PERFORMING DOGS, &c.

Comprising a Troupe of well-trained Animals, whose performance is simply marvellous; most suitable for Garden Parties, Schools, Institutes, Public Halls, &c. About one hour 3 3 0

PERFORMING BIRDS, CATS, AND MICE.

A Celebrated Troupe, Wonderfully Trained.—The Java Sparrow on the Tight Rope, Throwing Somersaults, Champagne Charlie fetching and carrying; Race with Birds, Steeplechasing over Gates and Rifle Drill; the two clever Cats in their Boxing Match, and Holding the Pole for their two little friends the White Mice, who have a Race for the Flags, Tight-Rope Walking, &c. The Birds now take a Drive in a Carriage Drawn and Driven by Birds. Gun Practice and Death and Burial of Poor Cock Robin. Suitable for Drawing-room, Garden Fêtes, School Treat, &c. ... ... from 1 5 0

N.B.—The Prices above quoted are for performances within a radius of 4 miles from HARROD'S STORES, LIMITED, cabs and travelling expenses being charged extra. Terms or outside radius and country by agreement.

GENERAL HIRE.

No. 22 DEPARTMENT—FIRST FLOOR.

NEGRO COMEDIANS, BANJOISTS, AND COMICAL SKETCH ARTISTES.

£ s. d.

Either single or in bands up to 20 performers. The Entertainment is of a superior kind, and quite free from any vulgarity; it is well suited for large Parties. Special arrangements for a larger number. Halls, Schools, and Fêtes. Each performer 1 1 0

MUSICAL CLOWNS AND JUGGLERS.

Two Grotesque and Eccentric Musicians, playing on 16 different instruments, suitable for Drawing-room or Large Hall ... 4 4 0

Musical Clowns and Blondin Donkey, with Juggling if required, very laughable and amusing, suitable for Drawing-room or Large Hall.

Two Artistes, 1 hour 2 15 0

1½ hours 3 10 0

2 " 4 4 0

Clown Juggling by Lady and Gentlemen.—A very clever, amusing, and interesting performance, suitable for Drawing-room, Public Halls, Garden Parties, &c. About 1 hour ... 2 12 6

Juggler, in Grotesque Costume, with Balls, Tops, Knives, Swords, Umbrellas, Balancing, &c.; a Novel Entertainment, suitable for Drawing-room, Schools, Halls, or Garden Parties, ½ hour ... from 1 11 6

1 hour 2 2 0

The Automatic Dwarf Comedian (Will Downes). Appears from an Egg, introducing Eccentric Songs and Dances, also novel Skirt Dancing, Eccentric and Refined Musical Act, playing on 6 different Instruments, balancing Fire at the same time, also introduces his wonderful Clown Dog, giving a good hour's diversion ... 4 4 0

With a pianist as accompanist 5 5 0

A Stage is required for this performance.

Edison's Phonograph, with latest improvements. Reproduces the newest Songs, Bands, Speeches, Recitations, Dialogues, &c. Suitable for At Homes, Conversaziones, Children's and Adult Parties, not exceeding 2 hours 2 2 0

For every half-hour or part thereof after 0 10 6

CONJURING.

By the most eminent Professors of the day. Introducing the latest Novelties, with Birds, Rabbits, Coins, Cards, Eggs, Handkerchiefs, Watches, Hats, &c. &c., and will be found most entertaining, either for the Drawing-room or the Public Stage, with strict regard to refinement.

No. 1. One hour's Simple Conjuring (no live stock) ... 1 1 0

" 2. " " with Superior Apparatus (ditto ditto) ... 1 17 6

" 3. " " attended by well-known Professor, and with Live Stock ... 2 12 6

" 4. One and a-half hour's Conjuring, adapted for Large Halls, Public Institutions, Drawing-room, &c. 3 3 0

" 5. Two hours superior Conjuring, with all the latest Novelties in the Magic Art, attended by one of the most eminent Professors of the day 4 4 0

N.B.—The Prices above quoted are for performances within a radius of 4 miles from HARROD'S STORES, LIMITED, cabs and travelling expenses being charged extra. Terms for outside radius and country by agreement.

Playing games

Stimulus material

- How to Play Charades, from *Enquire Within Upon Everything* (1884).

Background

Although it may be hard to imagine a world without television and games consoles, the Victorians had to entertain themselves without them. In the evenings, adults and children used to read, play music, play games and even talk to each other! Charades was a popular party game. The extract from *Enquire Within Upon Everything* explains how to play charades and gives 'the most comprehensive list of words ever published upon which charades may be founded'.

Suggeted activities

- Look at the list of suggested words from *Enquire Within Upon Everything*. Highlight some of the words that are no longer in common usage. Try to find out their meaning.
- Have a go at playing the game.

53. Charades (Acted).—A drawing room with folded doors is the best for the purpose. Various household appliances are employed to fit up something like a stage, and to supply the fitting scenes. Characters dressed in costumes made up of handkerchiefs, coats, shawls, table-covers, &c., come on and perform an extempore play, founded upon the parts of a word, and its *whole*, as indicated already. For instance, the events explained in the poem given might be *acted*—glasses might be rung for bells—something might be said in the course of the dialogues about the sound of the bells being delightful to the *ear*; there might be a dance of the villagers, in which a *ring* might be formed; a wedding might be performed; and so on: but for *acting charades* there are many better words, because *Ear-ring* could with difficulty be *re-presented* without at once betraying the meaning. There is a little work entitled "Philosophy and Mirth united by Pen and Pencil," and another work, "Our Charades," and How we Played Them,"* by Jean Francis, which supply a large number of these Charades. But the following is the most extensive list of words ever published upon which Charades may be founded:—

54. Words which may be converted into **Acting or Written Charades** :—

Aid-less, Air-pump, Ale-house, Ann-ounce, Arch-angel, Arm-let, Art-less, Ass-ail, Ba-boon, Back-bite, Back-slide, Bag-gage, Bag-pipe, Bag-dad, Ball-able, Bale-ful, Band-age, Band-box, Bane-ful, Bar-bed, Bar-gain, Bar-rack, Bar-row, Bat-ten, Beard-less, Bid-den, Bird-lime, Birth-right, Black-guard, Blame-less, Block-head, Boat-man, Boot-jack, Book-worm, Bound-less, Bow-ling, Brace-let, Brain-less, Break-fast,

Break-less, Brick-bat, Brick-dust, Bride-cake, Bride-groom, Brim-stone, Broad-cloth, Broad-side, Broad-sword, Brow-beat, Bug-bear, Bull-dog, Bump-kin, Buoy-ant, But-ton, Cab-in, Can-did, Can-ton, Care-ful, Car-pet, Cart-ridge, Chair-man, Chamber-maid, Cheer-ful, Cheer-less, Christ-mas, Church-yard, Clans-men, Clerk-ship, Cob-web, Cock-pit, Cod-ling, Coin-age, Con-fined, Con-firm, Con-form, Con-tent, Con-test, Con-tract, Con-verse, Cork-screw, Count-less, Court-ship, Crab-bed, Cross-bow, Cur-tail, Cut-throat, Dark-some, Day-break, Death-watch, Dog-ma, Don-key, Drink-able, Drug-get, Duck-ling, Ear-ring, Earth-quake,

Ear-wig, False-hood, Fan-atic, Far-well, Far-thing, Fear-less, Fee-ling, Field-fare, Fire-lock, Fire-sword, Fire-man, Fire-pan, Fire-ship, Fire-work, Fir-kin, Fish-hook, Foot-ball, Foot-pad, Foot-stool, Fond-ling, For-age, Fur-bear, Fur-bid, Found-ling, Fox-glove, Free-hold, Free-stone, Fret-work, Fri-day, Fiend-ship, Frost-bite, Fur-long, Gain-say, Gang-way, Glow-worm, Glut-ton, God-father, God-mother, God-daughter, God-son, God-like, God-child, Gold-finch, Gold-smith, Goose-berry, Grand-father, Grate-ful, Grave-stone, Green-finch, Grey-hound, Grim-ace, Grind-stone, Ground-oak, Ground-sel,

Guard-ship, Gun-powder, Had-dock, Hail-stone, Hail-storm, Half-penny, Ham-let, Ham-mock, Hand-cuff, Hang-man, Hap-pen, Hard-ship, Hard-ware, Hart-horn, Head-land, Head-less, Head-long, Head-stone, Head-strong, Hear-say, Heart-less, Heart-sick, Heart-string, Hedge-hog, Heir-less, Heir-loom, Hell-hound, Hell-kite, Hence-forth, Herb-age, Herb-stone, Herd-man, Her-self, Hid-den, High-land, High-way, Hind-most, Hoar-frost, Hob-goblin, Hog-head, Home-bred, Honey-bag, Honey-comb, Honey-moon, Honey-suckle, Hood-wink, Horse-back, Horse-shoe, Hot-age, Hot-bed, Hot-house, Hot-spur, Hound-ditch, Hour-glass, House-hold, House-maid, House-wife, Hum-drum,

Hump-back, Hurri-cane, Ill-nature, Ill-usage, In-action, In-born, In-crease, In-justice, Ink-ling, In-land, In-mate, In-no-cent, In-sane, In-spirit, In-tent, Inter-meddle, Inter-sect, Inter-view, In-valid, In-vent, In-ward, Ire-ful, Iron-mould, I-sing-lass, Jack-ky-bite, Joy-ful, Joy-less, Justice-ship, Key-stone, Kid-nap, King-craft, King-fisher, Kins-man, Knight-hood, Know-ledge, Lace-man, Lady-bird, Lady-ship, Lamp-black, Land-bred, Land-lady, Land-lord, Land-mark, Land-scape, Land-tax, Lap-dog, Lap-pet, Land-able, Law-giver, Law-suit, Lay-man, Leap-frog, Leap-year, Lee-ward, Life-guard, Like-wise, Live-long,

Load-stone, Leg-book, Leg-wood, Loop-hole, Lord-ship, Love-sick, Low-land, Luck-less, Luke-warm, Ma-caw, Mad-cap, Mad-den, Mad-man, Mag-pie, Main-mast, Main-sail, Main-spring, Mam-moth, Man-date, Man-stan, Mark-man, Mar-row, Mass-acre, Match-less, May-game, Meat-man, Mis-chance, Mis-chief, Mis-count, Mis-deed, Mis-judge, Mis-quote, Moon-light, Monks-hood, Moon-beam, Muf-fin, Name-sake, Nau-keen, Nap-kin, Neck-lace, Neck-cloth, Nest-ling, News-paper, Nick-name, Night-cap, Night-gown, Night-mare, Night-watch, Nine-fold, Noon-tide, North-star, North-ward, Not-able, Not-ice, No-where, Nut-gall, Nut-meg, Oak-apple,

Oat-cake, Oat-meal, Off-end, Oil-man, O-men, On-set, O-pen, O-pinion, Over-act, Over-awe, Over-bear, Over-boil, Over-board, Over-burden, Over-cast, Over-charge, Over-cloud, Over-come, Over-court, Over-do, Over-due, Over-eye, Over-feed, Over-flow, Over-grown, Over-head, Over-hear, Over-hand, Over-joy, Over-lade, Over-lay, Over-leap, Over-load, Over-look, Over-mast, Over-match, Over-right, Over-pass, Over-pay, Over-peer, Over-plus, Over-poise, Over-power, Over-press, Over-rack, Over-reach, Over-rule, Over-ripen, Over-roast, Over-run, Over-see, Over-set, Over-shade, Over-shoe, Over-bud,

Over-sight, Over-size, Over-sleep, Over-spread, Over-stock, Over-strain, Over-away, Over-swell, Over-take, Over-throw, Over-took, Over-value, Over-work, Our-selves, Out-act, Out-bid, Out-brave, Out-brazen, Out-cast, Out-cry, Out-do, Out-grow, Out-law, Out-line, Out-live, Out-march, Out-rage, Out-ride, Out-run, Out-sail, Out-shine, Out-side, Out-sit, Out-sleep, Out-spread, Out-stare, Out-right, Out-stretch, Out-talk, Out-via, Out-ward, Out-weigh, Out-wit, Out-work, Ox-gall, Ox-lip, Pack-age, Pack-cloth, Pad-dock, Pad-lock, Pain-ful, Pain-less, Pal-ace, Pal-et, Pan-cake, Pan-tiles,

Pa-pa, Par-able, Par-pal, Par-rent, Pa-ring, Par-ship, Par-son, Par-took, Part-ridge, Pass-over, Past-time, Patch-work, Pa-tent, Path-way, Peer-age, Peer-less, Pen-knife, Pen-man, Pen-man-ship, Penny-worth, Per-jury, Port-in-a-city, Pick-lock, Pick-pocket, Fire-bald, Fire-staff, Pike-staff, Pin-cushion, Pine-apple, Pip-kin, Pitch-fork, Pit-men, Plain-tiff, Play-fellow, Play-house, Play-mate, Play-wright, Plough-man, Plough-share, Pole-cat, Po-lute, Pop-gun, Pop-in-jay, Port-able, Port-hole, Post-age, Post-chaise, Post-date, Post-house, Post-office, Pot-ash, Pot-book,

Pound-age, Prim-rose, Prior-ship, Prop-a-gate, Punch-bowl, Quad-rant, Quench-less, Quick-lime, Quick-sand, Quick-set, Quick-silver, Rain-bow, Ram-part, Ran-sack, Rap-a-city, Rasp-berry, Rattle-snake, Red-breast, Red-cock, Pear-led, Peer-age, Rid-dance, Ring-leader, Ring-let, Ring-tail, Ring-worm, Rolling-pin, Rose-water, Rot-ten, Round-about, Round-house, Run-a-gate, Rush-light, Safe-guard, Sal-low, Sand-stone, Sat-in, Sat-ire, Sauce-box, Sauce-pan, Saw-dust, Saw-pit, Scare-crow, Scarf-skin, Scar-let, School-fellow, School-master, School-mistress, Silk-weaver, Silk-worm, Silver-smith, Sin-less, Sir-fold, Skim-milk, Skip-jack, Sky-jack, Sky-light, Slap-dash, Sleeve-less, Slip-board, Slip-shod,

Seam-stress, Sea-nymph, Sea-port, Sea-son, Sea-ward, Second-hand, Seed-cake, Sod-den, Seed-ling, Seed-pearl, Seed-time, Sex-tile, Sex-ton, Shame-less, Shame-rock, Shape-less, Sharp-set, Sheep-cot, Sheep-shearing, Sheep-walk, Steel-anchor, Shell-fish, Shift-less, Ship-board, Ship-wreck, Shirt-less, Shoe-maker, Shore-maker, Shop-board, Shop-keeper, Shop-man, Shore-less, Short-hand, Short-lived, Short-sighted, Shot-free, Shoulder-belt, Shrove-tide, Side-board, Side-long, Side-saddle, Side-ways, Sight-less,

Slip-slop, Slope-wise, Slow-worm, Snip-pet, Snow-ball, Snow-drop, Son-less, Sup-plant, Sod-den, Sol-ace, So-lo, Sol-rent, Sup-port-able, Sup-position, Sup-press, Swan-down, Sweep-stake, Sweet-bread, Sweet-briar, Sweet-heart, Sweet-william, Sweet-willow, Swine-herd, Swords-man, Span-king, Spare-rib, Spar-row, Speak-able, Speech-less, Sports-man, Spot-less, Spite-ful, Spring-halt, Spruce-beer, Stair-case, Stair-at, Star-gazer, Star-light, Star-like, States-man, Stead-fast, Steel-yard, Steep-age, Step-dame, Step-daughter, Step-father, Step-mother, Steward-ship, Still-neck, Stiff-neck, Stock-jobber, Stone-fruit, Store-fruit, Store-house, Stow-age, Strata-gem, Straw-berry, Stream-let, Stream-fold, Strip-ling, Summer-house,

Sum-mary, Summer-set, Sun-beam, Sun-burnt, Sun-day, Sun-dry, Sun-flower, Son-less, Sup-plant, Sol-ace, So-lo, Sol-rent, Sup-port-able, Sup-position, Sup-press, Swan-down, Sweep-stake, Sweet-bread, Sweet-briar, Sweet-heart, Sweet-william, Sweet-willow, Swine-herd, Swords-man, Tar-get, Taw-dry, Tax-able, Tea-cup, Term-ful, Term-less, Tell-tale, Ten-a-city, Ten-ant, Ten-dance, Ten-don, Ten-dril, Ten-or, Thank-ful, Thank-less, Them-selves, Thence-forth, There-after, There-at, There-by, There-fore, There-from, There-in, There-on, There-to, There-with, Thick-set, Thought-ful, Thought-less, Thread-bare, Thread-gem, Three-fold, Three-score, Thresh-wd,

Through-out, Thunder-struck, Thunder-bolt, Till-age, Tip-pet, Tip-staff, Tire-some, Title-page, Toad-stool, Toll-some, Turn-boy, Tooth-ache, Top-knot, Top-most, Top-sail, Touch-stone, Touch-wood, Towns-man, Toy-shop, Trap-door, Tre-foil, Trip-thong, Trip-let, Trod-den, Turn-pike, Turn-spit, Turn-stile, Tutor-age, Twelfth-tide, Twelfth-night, Two-fold, Two-pence,

Up-shot, Up-ride, Up-start, Up-ward, Up-bill, Up-bold, Up-braid, Up-land, Up-right, Up-rose, Vain-glory, Van-guard, Vault-age, Wag-on, Wag-tail, Wain-coat, Wain-scot, Wal-nut, Wan-ton, Ward-robe, Ward-ship, Ward-mote, Ware-house, War-fare, War-like, War-rant, Wash-ball, Waste-ful, Watch-ful,

Watch-man, Watch-word, Water-course, Water-fall, Water-fowl, Water-mark, Water-man, Water-mill, Water-work, Way-ward, Way-lay, Weather-cock, Weather-glass, Weather-wise, Web-bed, Web-foot, Wed-lock, Week-day, Wel-come, Wel-fare, Well-born, Well-bred, Wheel-wright, Where-at, Where-by, Whet-stone, Whip-cord, Whip-hand, Whirl-pool, Whirl-wind, White-wind, White-wash, Whit-low, Whit-sun-tide, Who-ever, Whole-sale, Whole-some, Wil-low, Wind-fire, Wind-lass, Wind-mill, Wind-pipe, Win-now, Wise-acre, Wit-less, Wolf-dog, Wood-cock, Wood-lark, Wood-man, Wood-nole, Wood-nymph, Work-house, Wor-sted, Worm-wood, Wrath-ful, Wrist-band, Writ-ten, Year-ling, Youth-ful.

Nursery rhymes

Stimulus material

Nursery Rhymes: *Punch*, 10 January 1863.

Background

For a time, *Punch* magazine published short, humorous rhymes about the inhabitants of towns and villages. Today, these kinds of poems are often known as limericks. *Punch* stated its intention to continue to publish these poems 'until every town has been immortalised'.

Suggested activities

- Find the names of some towns and villages on a map of your own area.
- Make a list of some of them and then see how many rhyming words you can find for each one.
- Choose a place with plenty of rhyming opportunities and aim to write a poem similar to the examples from *Punch*.

NURSERY RHYMES.

(To be continued until every Town in the Kingdom has been immortalised.)

HERE was a young lady of Poole,
Who thought she would set up a school;
But all she could teach
Were the nine parts of speech,
And how to make gooseberry fool.

There was a young lady of Deal,
Who ate up five platefulls of veal,
A sausage, and ham,
And some raspberry jam,
And said, "I have made a good meal."

There was a young lady of Skye,
Who declared she was going to die,
But was instantly cured
When politely assured
If she did, there was no one would cry.

There was a young lady of Oakham,
Who would steal your cigars and then soak 'em
  In treacle and rum,
  And then smear them with gum;
So it wasn't a pleasure to smoke 'em.

There was a young lady of Crewe,
Whose eyes were excessively blue;
  So she got an old fellow
  To rub them with yellow,
And so they turned green; which is true.

There was a young lady of Cirencester,
She went to consult a solicitor,
  When he wanted his fee,
  She said "Fiddledeedee,
I only looked in as a visitor."

Punch, 10 January 1863

Lost and found

Stimulus material
- Advertisements from *The Times*, 6 May 1852, 22 May 1852 and 1 January 1861.

Background

Unlike today, the front page of *The Times* was devoted to advertisements. Opposite is a reproduction of the lost and found column. You may notice that three of the advertisements are for lost people!

Suggested activities
- Look at the advertisements carefully. Notice that the first few words are in bold type to attract attention.
- Write a 'lost' advertisement describing something precious to you. This might be a pet, a favourite toy or even a member of your family! Remember to describe the lost item/person, saying where and when it/she/he was last seen and give an address to where it should be returned. You may want to offer a reward. Aim to use the whole width of the column so that your work can be pasted onto a large sheet with others to reproduce the column from a newspaper.

Extension activities
- You may have time to write an imaginative 'found' advertisement.

LEDA.—Michael Angelo.—Mr. D—N is requested to CALL on or COMMUNICATE with H.—May, 1852.

LEFT his HOME, on Monday, April 26, a YOUTH, aged 17. Had on a dark speckled coat, old dark blue cloth waistcoat, cord trousers, light blue cap with a peak, low shoes, gray lamb's-wool stockings marked T. W., grocer's apron fringed at top; scar on the back of right hand, brown mark on his left elbow, dark hair, small light blue eyes, fair complexion, treads out with his left foot. Any information will be thankfully received by Mr. Wilson, grocer, Croydon (Old-town). If he sees this, he is begged to return to his distressed parents.

LOST, on the 4th inst., a small GOLD CHATELAINE, with appendages (one being a peculiar old coin), either in Baker-street, or between there and Conduit-street. Whoever will bring it to Mr. Jeans, bookseller, High-street, St. John's-wood, shall be liberally REWARDED.

LOST, on Tuesday night, between 11 and 12, off a Chelsea and Hoxton omnibus, between the Sturt Arms and Worship-street, a CANE, with ivory hook and gold mount. Whoever has found it and will bring it to 60, Chandos-street, Covent-garden, will be amply REWARDED.—May 5.

LOST, on Tuesday morning, between Sussex-terrace, Hyde-park, and Baker-street Bazaar, by way of Chester-place and Berkeley-street, a LADY's GOLD HUNTING WATCH, with chain and appendages. Whoever has found the same, and will bring them to Mr. Calder's library, 1, Bathurst-street, Sussex-square, shall receive TWO GUINEAS REWARD.

LOST MONEY.—FORTY-FIVE POUNDS have been received in a blank envelope, with no clue to the sender. It consists of a bank post bill and two notes, and is supposed to have been transmitted by mistake. The owner may recover the same on giving satisfactory proof of having a just claim. Apply to Mr. Wright, bookseller to the Queen, 60, Pall-mall.

TEN GUINEAS REWARD.—LOST, on the 29th April, 1852, between the Bank and General Post-office, a SET of ARTIFICIAL TEETH, in a morocco case; on the plates are stamped the name of Jarritt and Canton, dentists, 34, Poultry. Whoever has found the same, and will leave them at J. Weekes, Esq.'s, surgeon, High-street, Bloomsbury; or at Jarritt and Canton's, dentists, Poultry, shall receive the above reward.

TWO GUINEAS REWARD.—LOST, in Paris, in March, 1851, a BANK POST BILL for £10, C 3,225, March 10, 1851. Whoever will bring the same to 4, Hyde-park-square, shall receive the above reward.

FOUND, a ROLL of BANK of ENGLAND NOTES. Whoever has lost the same can have them by applying for them and paying expenses, and giving a full description of them, to A. H., 38, Great Castle-street, Regent-street.

FOUND, a GOLD DIAMOND RING, with an inscription on it. Whoever has lost the same may have it by giving a proper description, and paying the expenses incurred, on application to Miss Linnell, milliner, 18, High-street, Notting-hill.

FOUND, on Wednesday, April 28, at Ewell, Surrey, a POINTER DOG. The owner can have it by applying at the Cottage, Cheam, Surrey. If not claimed in 10 days it will be

LEFT his HOME, about 9 o'clock on the evening of Tuesday last, May 18, a YOUTH, 15 years of age, of fair complexion, hair, and eyes, about 5 feet 5 inches in height. He had with him a small green carpet bag, containing wearing apparel, and was dressed in a reddish brown Scotch tweed shooting coat at the time he left. Information of his recovery to be addressed to the Inspector of Police, Eltham, Kent.

BOY LOST.—LOST, on Tuesday, 11th May, 1852, Wm. BIRD, eleven years of age, small in stature, and of fair complexion, with a scar on his forehead. Had on corduroy trousers, a blue cotton coat, light waistcoat, cloth cap, and a brown silk neckerchief, with a new pair of laced boots. Any tidings of him will be thankfully received by his friends, at 13, Tyssen-road, Stoke Newington.

LOST, a HORSEHAIR RETICULE, containing a lava brooch, on the 19th ultimo, near Bishopsgate Church. Whoever will bring the same to Mr C. H. Palmer, 55, Gracechurch-street, will receive a REWARD of TEN SHILLINGS.

LOST, a PHOTOGRAPHIC PORTRAIT of a LADY, in morocco case. The finder, on leaving it at Wilson and Sons', 103, Cheapside, shall receive FIVE SHILLINGS REWARD.

TEN POUNDS REWARD.—LOST, on the evening of the 19th of May, a GOLD WATCH: maker's name French, No. 7,827. Whoever will bring the same to Mr. French, Royal Exchange, will receive the above reward.

THREE POUNDS REWARD.—LOST, on Thursday, the 13th inst., between Stanhope-street and Hyde-park-corner-gate, a TWISTED GOLD CHAIN BRACELET, with three lockets containing hair attached to it; engraved with initials. Whoever brings it to Mr. Taking's, 48, Curzon-street, will receive the above reward.

FIVE POUNDS REWARD.—LOST, between Temple-bar and Baker street, on Friday, the 21st inst. BANK NOTES for £50, numbered 89,291 to 89,300, dated 1st April, 1852. Whoever will bring the same to Mr. F. Waller, 49, Fleet-street, shall receive the above reward. Payment of the notes has been stopped at the Bank.

MYSTERIOUSLY DISAPPEARED, a YOUNG LADY, from Hawkhurst, Kent. The utmost publicity will be given unless immediate communication is made to her relatives.—C. F. Field (late Chief Inspector of the Detective Police), 20, Devereux-court, Temple, Private Inquiry-office, 31st December, 1860.

LOST, on Wednesday last, the 27th, a CANE, bearing the inscription " Better than the other." Whoever will bring the same to 9, Norfolk-square, Paddington, shall receive TEN SHILLINGS REWARD.

LOST, Dec. 24, a GOLD WATCH KEY, Chain, and Seal, set with turquoise, between Langley-broom, Slough, and Woodcot, Goring. ONE POUND REWARD. The finder will please address or bring to Mr. Channon, post-office, Brompton-row, London, S.W.

LOST, on Friday, the 28th ult., in the neighbourhood of the Blackfriars-road, a GOLD BREAST PIN, two rows of diamonds and sapphire in centre. TEN POUNDS REWARD will be paid on recovery. Information to 4, Kennington-row, Kennington-common.

LOST (FIVE POUNDS REWARD), on the 18th December last, in the neighbourhood of New-square, Lincoln's-inn, a LADY's GOLD WATCH. Information to Charles Frederick Field (late Chief Inspector of the Detective Police), 20, Devereux-court, Temple, Private Inquiry-office.—31st December, 1860.

LOST, on the evening of the 27th December, at Pimlico, a LETTER, addressed " — Weldon, Esq., Manager of London and Westminster Bank," and containing two crossed cheques and a note, payment of which has been stopped. Any person returning the same to Mr. Clarke, advertising agent, 51, Threadneedle-street, E.C., shall be handsomely REWARDED.

LOST, at about 2 o'clock, on Monday afternoon, Dec. 10, 1860, between the Butcher Market and High Villa-place, Newcastle-upon-Tyne, EIGHT new £5 NOTES of the BANK of ENGLAND. The notes were in a drab cotton bag, with red braid string. The numbers of the notes are 04834, 04835, 04836, 04837, 04838, 04839, 04840, 04841, dated Newcastle-upon-Tyne, 11th August, 1860, and are stopped at the Bank. Whoever will return the same to the police station, Westgate, Newcastle-upon-Tyne, will be handsomely REWARDED.—Dec. 13, 1860.

TWO POUNDS REWARD.—Payment Stopped at the Bank.—LOST, on Saturday evening last, TWO BANK of ENGLAND NOTES, of £5, numbers 82,274-5. Apply at 53, Manchester-street, Manchester-square.

TEN SHILLINGS REWARD.—STRAYED, on Friday evening last, a CAT, colour light gray, with a collar and lock on. If she is brought to 11, Hyde-park-street, the above sum will be paid.

ONE SOVEREIGN REWARD.—LOST, in Bond-street, December 28, about half past 5 p.m, a small SCOTCH TERRIER, black muzzle. Name " Snap." To be brought to Mr. Maddox, stationer, Albany-street, Regent's-park.

FIVE POUNDS REWARD.—LOST, in the neighbourhood of the west-end, on the 22d ult., a SQUARE PARCEL in white paper, containing a gold bracelet, a jet bracelet, and a sovereign. Whoever will bring the above to 291, Regent-street, shall receive the above reward.

TEN POUNDS REWARD.—LOST, a DIAMOND PENDANT BROOCH, supposed to have been dropped in a cab, on Christmas night, between Chesham-street, Belgravia, and Upper Ranelagh-street, or from Upper Ranelagh-street and the Euston Hotel. Apply to the Manager, Euston Hotel.

Situations vacant

Stimulus material

- *The Times* newspaper, Situations Vacant: Advertising for servants.

Suggested activities

- Write an advertisement to attract a servant to work in your house. You will need to explain their duties and describe the sort of person that you are looking for. Remember to give an address for replies.

- Imagine that you are looking for a position in service. Write a reply to one of the advertisements. Give some details about yourself. Explain why you think that you are suitable for the job.

- Write a list of interview questions to ask the applicants who have responded to your advertisement. Work with a partner to act out the interview itself.

Extension activity

- Imagine that the new servant is unsatisfactory. Work out a script to show the conversation between the employer and the servant.

WANTED, in a small, quiet family (where no footman is kept), two miles from Oxford-street, a respectable woman, about 30 years of age, as thorough good PLAIN COOK. She must have a good character from her last situation for cleanliness and sobriety. (No crinoline allowed.) Letters, stating age, directed to G. L., 49, Salisbury-street, Lisson-grove. Wages £14, with tea and sugar.

WANTED, a PAGE.—A gentleman is in WANT of a YOUTH duly qualified to wait at table, clean plate, and perform the usual duties of that situation. One who can be well recommended will be preferred. Apply by letter to J. R., at Ravensfell, Bromley, Kent; or personally at 17, St. Helen's-place, Bishopsgate-street (ground floor), between 11 and 1, any day except Wednesday.

WANTED, a good PLAIN COOK, by a family residing in the neighbourhood of London. She must understand the management of a small dairy. To a conscientious, trustworthy person the place would prove a comfortable one. A kitchenmaid is kept. Apply by letter to M. O., care of Messrs. Davies and Co., advertising agents, 1, Finch-lane, Cornhill.

WANTED, for a private family, THREE good active SERVANTS—a very good Plain Cook, who will not object to do a portion of the housework; a Housemaid, of respectable appearance and manner, who will be required to wait at table; and a Nurse, to wash and dress four children (the youngest four years old), and to clean the nurseries. French or German not objected to for the nurse. The washing is all put out, and good wages will be given to useful efficient servants. No other servants kept. Apply at Mr. Bolton's newspaper-office, Knightsbridge.

WANTED, a PARTNER, with £6,000, in an old-established brewery, in a large sea-port town, adapted to home and export trade. The keeping properties of the ales are superior, and (combined with the excellent quality of the water) a first-class article is produced, as well as ale, equal to Burton ales. The advertiser invites the strictest inquiry, and feeling confident of the remunerating returns of the concern, he stipulates for the same from applicants. Apply to A. B., care of Messrs. Chester, Toulmin, and Chester, 11, Staple-inn, London.

WANTED, a good GENERAL SERVANT, for a small private family. She must be a good plain cook, kind and obliging, willing to occasionally assist in the nursery, and have an undeniable character for honesty, sobriety, cleanliness, &c. Family's washing put out. Wages £12, and everything found. Also, for the same family, a respectable young woman, of good temper and habits (who is fond of, and understands the management of, young children), as Nursemaid. She must have a good character for honesty, sobriety, cleanliness, &c., and work well at her needle. Wages £10, and everything found. Apply this day at 7, Stamford-grove east, Hill-street, Upper Clapton.

The Times, 1 June 1861

Posters

Stimulus material
- Stolen/Reward poster for FA Cup, 1895.

Background

After winning the FA cup in 1895, Aston Villa Football Club allowed it to be displayed in the window of a shop belonging to William Shillcock. On the night of 11 September that year, the cup was stolen. Although a reward of £10 was offered for its safe return, the cup was never found. In 1958, 83-year-old Harry Bridge told a newspaper that he had stolen it and used it to make false coins. Another man called John 'Stosher' Stait also claimed that he had been the thief.

Suggested activities
- What do you think happened to the cup? Why do you think two separate people claimed to have committed the crime? Perhaps neither of them did it!
- Write an imaginary letter of confession. Explain why you wanted the cup, how you managed to steal it and what you did with it.
- Imagine that you are a barrister trying to solve the mystery. Write a set of questions to be put to the suspects. Your friends could act the parts of Harry Bridge, John Stait and any other suspects. Act out your interviews. Your audience could act as a jury.

£10 REWARD.

STOLEN!

From the Shop Window of W. Shillcock, Football
Outfitter, Newtown Row, Birmingham, between the
hour of 9-30 p.m. on Wednesday, the 11th September,
and 7-30 a.m., on Thursday, the 12th inst., the

ENGLISH CUP,

the property of Aston Villa F.C. The premises
were broken into between the hours named, and the
Cup, together with cash in drawer, stolen.

The above Reward will be paid for the recovery
of the Cup, or for information as may lead to the
conviction of the thieves.

Information to be given to the Chief of Police,
or to Mr. W. Shillcock, 73, Newtown Row.

Hints for home comfort

Stimulus material

- The Regulation of Domestic Affairs: Hints for Home Comfort and Household Management, from *Enquire Within Upon Everything* (1884).

Background

Many Victorians were keen to share thrifty ideas and other household tips. Some of these were published in the pages of books and magazines such as *Enquire Within Upon Everything*.

Suggested activities

- Read the advice given in the extracts from *Enquire Within Upon Everything*.
- In your group, compile your own list of hints or rules for home comfort, safety and household management. You might be able to include advice given to you by the adults you live with, for example advice about hanging up clothes, leaving shoes tidily, turning lights off, etc.

474. Hints for Home Comfort.

i. Eat slowly and you will not over-eat.

ii. Keeping the feet warm will prevent headaches.

iii. Late at breakfast—hurried for dinner—cross at tea.

iv. A short needle makes the most expedition in plain sewing.

v. Between husband and wife little attentions beget much love.

vi. Always lay your table neatly, whether you have company or not.

vii. Put your balls or reels of cotton into little bags, leaving the ends out.

viii. Whatever you may choose to give away, always be sure to *keep your temper*.

ix. Dirty windows speak to the passer-by of the negligence of the inmates.

x. In cold weather a leg of mutton improves by being hung three, four, or five weeks.

xi. When meat is hanging, change its position frequently, to equally distribute the juices.

xii. There is much more injury done by admitting visitors to invalids than is generally supposed.

xiii. Matches, out of the reach of children, should be kept in every bed-room. They are cheap enough.

xiv. Apple and suet dumplings are lighter when boiled in a net than a cloth. Skim the pot well.

xv. When sheets or chamber towels get thin in the middle, cut them in two, sew the selvedges together, and hem the sides.

xvi. When you are particular in wishing to have precisely what you want from a butcher, go and buy it yourself.

xvii. A flannel petticoat will wear as nearly as long again, if turned hind part before, when the front begins to wear thin.

xviii. People in general are not aware how very essential to the health of the inmates is the free admission of light into their houses.

xix. When you dry salt for the table, do not place it in the salt cellars until it is cold, otherwise it will harden into a lump.

xx. Never put away plate, knives and forks, &c., uncleaned, or great inconvenience will arise when the articles are wanted.

xxi. Feather beds should be opened every third year, the ticking well dusted, soaped, and waxed, the feathers dressed and returned.

xxii. Persons of defective sight, when threading a needle, should hold it over something white, by which the sight will be assisted.

xxiii. In mending sheets and shirts, put in pieces sufficiently large, or in the first washing the thin parts give way, and the work done is of no avail.

xxiv. When reading by candle-light, place the candle behind you, that the rays may pass over your shoulder on to the book. This will relieve the eyes.

xxv. A wire fire-guard, for each fire-place in a house, costs little, and greatly diminishes the risk to life and property. Fix them before going to bed.

xxvi. In winter, get the work forward by daylight, to prevent running about at night with candles. Thus you escape grease spots, and risks of fire.

xxvii.—Be at much pains to keep your children's feet dry and warm. Don't bury their bodies in heavy flannels and wools, and leave their arms and legs naked.

438. A Hint on Household Management.

—Have you ever observed what a dislike servants have to anything cheap? They hate saving their master's money. I tried this experiment with great success the other day. Finding we consumed a vast deal of soap, I sat down in my thinking chair, and took the soap question into consideration, and I found reason to suspect we were using a very expensive article, where a much cheaper one would serve the purpose better. I ordered half a dozen pounds of both sorts, but took the precaution of changing the papers on which the prices were marked before giving them into the hands of Betty. "Well, Betty, which soap do you find washes best?" "Oh, please sir, the dearest, in the blue paper; it makes a lather as well again as the other." "Well, Betty, you shall always have it then;" and thus the unsuspecting Betty saved me some pounds a year, and washed the clothes better—*Rev. Sydney Smith*.

Words of wisdom

Stimulus material
Words of Wisdom from *Enquire Within Upon Everything* (1884).

Background
Enquire Within Upon Everything was a household guide on a wide variety of subjects ranging from advice on how to get married to what to do in the event of a carriage crash. At the top of each page are 'words of wisdom' designed to encourage readers to lead a healthy, happy and honest lifestyle.

Suggested activities
- Read the copied extracts. Aim to categorise them under the following titles:

    Advice on being truthful/honest/kind/modest.

    Warnings against bad deeds/acts.

    Reminders to be kind/honest/good.

    Reminders about working hard.

    Advice on staying healthy.

    Advice on staying out of debt/living within one's means.

    Advice that does not fit into other catagories.

    Then cut and paste or copy them onto the grid provided.
- Make up some more 'Words of Wisdom' for this century. They might, for example, be about mobile phones, driving manners, bed-times, etc.

VICTORIAN WORDS OF WISDOM

Advice on being truthful/honest/kind/modest	Warnings against bad deeds/acts	Reminders to be kind/honest/good	Advice on staying healthy	Advice on staying out of debt	Advice that does not fit other categories

To be enlarged to A3 size

Excess calls in the doctor.

Eat not to dullness,
drink not to elevation.

Disease is soon shaken
by physic soon taken.

Disease is the punishment of neglect.

Keep the blood pure and spare the leech.

Loose habits lead to bandages.

Bottles of brandy are followed
by bottles of physic.

Be temperate in all things.

Keep the head cool and the feet warm.

Guard the foot
and the head will seldom harm.

Health is the reward of cleanliness.

Despise school and remain a fool.

A spark may raise an awful blaze.

Good nature collects honey
from every herb;
Ill-nature sucks poison
from the sweetest flower.

Deep rivers run with silent majesty;
Shallow brooks are noisy.

When angry, count ten before you speak.
If very angry, a hundred.

Never trouble another
for what you can do yourself.

Never put off until to-morrow
what you can do today.

A good beginning makes a good ending.

When we think we fail,
we are often near success.

Second trials often succeed.

Second thoughts are often best.

Observation is the best teacher.

Falsehood, like a nettle,
stings those who meddle with it.

Let truth be our guide.

If you are in debt,
someone owns part of you.

Economy is the easy chair of old age.

Avoid yourself what you think wrong
in your neighbours.

He that plays with fire may be burnt.

Walk swiftly from temptation
or it may overtake you.

A stitch in time saves nine.

Thrive by honesty or remain poor.

Use a book as a bee does a flower.

A good book is a light to the soul.

Every day in your life is a page in your history.

Perseverance overcomes difficulties.

A good word is as soon said as an ill one.

One kind word may
turn aside a torrent of anger.

The early bird catches the worm.

Time and tide tarry for no man.

An hour in the morning
is worth two at night.

Morning for work,
evening for contemplation.

Better to go to bed supperless
than to rise in debt.

Haste makes waste.

They must hunger in frost
those who will not work in heat.

Envy is a self-executioner.

The mill cannot grind
with water that is past.

Prevention is better than cure.

Never open the door to a little vice,
Lest a great one should enter also.

The windows opened more
would keep doctors from the door.

A dirty grate makes dinner late.

Too much bed makes a dull head.

A bad broom leaves a dirty room.

Do good to your enemy,
that he may become your friend.
Do good to your friend,
that he may remain your friend.

A liar should have a good memory.

Begin well and end better.

Night is not dark to the good,
Nor is day bright to the wicked.

Who never tries cannot win the prize.

The best physicians are Dr Diet,
Dr Quiet and Dr. Merryman.

Bustle is not industry.

A pleasant stay?

Stimulus material
- Advertisements for hotel accommodation.

Background
'Modern' Victonan hotels offered the luxury of electric lights and separate dining tables! Advertisements sometimes carried extracts from letters from satisfied customers.

Suggested activities
- Read the example advertisements. Imagine that you have been a paying guest in these hotels. Did they live up to the advertisements?
- Make some comments that you could have written in the visitors' book on the day of your departure. Try to relate them to the attractions listed in the advertisement for each hotel.

Name of hotel: VISITOR'S BOOK

Names of guests	Comments

Name of hotel: VISITOR'S BOOK

Names of guests	Comments

Extension activity
- Write a testimonal letter or letter of complaint to the manager of one of these hotels.

Disasters

Stimulus material

- Picture of the collapse of the Dale Dyke Dam.
- Painting of a dog next to a child floating in a crib, a brass dog collar and copy of the inscription on the collar.

Background

On 11 March 1864, a workman called William Horsefield was walking across the newly constructed Dale Dyke Dam eight miles north-west of Sheffield. To his horror he discovered a crack in the dam and he immediately went to tell John Gunson, the chief engineer of the waterworks.

Mr Gunson ordered that the water level in the lake behind the dam should be reduced, but that night the dam suddenly collapsed, causing millions of litres of water to rush down the valley in a huge and devastating wave.

The waters caused the collapse of houses and factories, and many people were swept from their beds. Tragically, 250 people lost their lives.

Ever since the disaster, amazing survival stories of a lucky few have been told. One story tells of a mother, father and their five children who floated on a bed until the waters subsided. Another story tells how a dog rescued a baby who had been floating in its cradle in the floodwaters.

No one seems to know for sure whether these survival stories are accurate. However, a brass collar still exists carrying an inscription that states that it belonged to a dog called Rollo. The inscription suggests that it was bought with money donated by others and it is dated 12 March – the day after the flood. Some people think that Rollo must have been the dog that rescued the baby. What do you think?

Suggested activities

- Produce a story board that shows the main events in the flood disaster story. You might wish to concentrate on one of the survival stories mentioned above.
- Imagine that you were an eye-witness to some of the events on 11 March 1864. Produce a piece of descriptive writing to describe what happened.

THIS COLLAR WAS PURCHASED BY
SUBSCRIPTION AND PRESENTED TO
"ROLLO"
THE PROPERTY OF MR. C. WALKER
PHILADELPHIA STEELWORKS
MARCH 12 1864

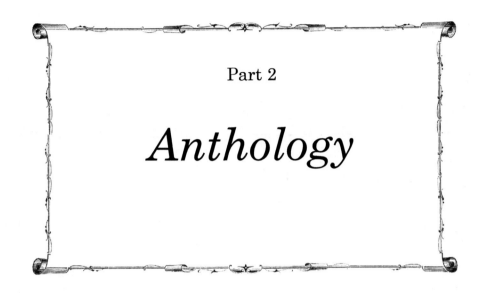

Part 2

Anthology

Dotheboys Hall

It was such a crowded scene, and there were so many objects to attract attention that, at first, Nicholas stared about him, really without seeing anything at all. By degrees, however, the place resolved itself into a bare and dirty room, with a couple of windows, whereof a tenth part might be of glass, the remainder being stopped up with old copy-books and paper. There were a couple of long old rickety desks, cut and notched, and inked, and damaged in every possible way; two or three forms; a detached desk for Squeers (the schoolmaster) and another for his assistant. The ceiling was supported, like that of a barn, by cross-beams and rafters; and the walls were so stained and discoloured that it was impossible to tell whether they had ever been touched with paint or whitewash.

But the pupils – the young noblemen! How the last faint traces of hope, the remotest glimmering of any good to be derived from his efforts in this den, faded from the mind of Nicholas as he looked in dismay around! Pale and haggard faces, lank and bony figures, children with the countenances of old men, deformities with irons upon their limbs, boys of stunted growth, and others whose long meagre legs would hardly bear their stooping bodies, all crowded on the view together. There were little faces which should have been handsome, darkened with the scowl of sullen, dogged suffering; there was childhood with the light of its eye quenched, its beauty gone, and its helplessness alone remaining; there were vicious-faced boys, brooding, with leaden eyes, like malefactors in jail.

(From *Nicholas Nickleby* by Charles Dickens)

A Victorian school

. . . The child looked round the room as she took her seat. There were a couple of forms (benches), notched and cut and inked all over; a small desk perched on four legs, at which no doubt the master sat; a few dog's-eared books upon a high shelf; and beside them a motley collection of peg-tops, balls, kites, fishing-lines, marbles, half-eaten apples, and other confiscated property of idle urchins.

Displayed on hooks upon the wall in all their terrors were the cane and ruler; and near them, on a shelf of its own, the dunce's cap, made of old newspapers and decorated with glaring wafers of the largest size. But, the great ornaments of the walls were certain moral sentences fairly copied in good round text and well-worked sums in simple addition and multiplication wafers – thin leaves of dry coloured paste used as seals

(From *The Old Curiosity Shop* by Charles Dickens)

Rules . . .

**To be observed by the Parents of Children attending
the National School at . . .**

Parents who wish to get their children admitted into the above-named
school, may do so by applying to the Master on any Monday morning,
at a quarter before 9 o'clock.

Parents are requested to pay particular attention to the following
rules:

1. The children are to assemble at the school on every week-day morning at a quarter before 9, and every afternoon at a quarter before 2 o'clock, except Saturday, which is a holiday.
2. On the Sunday the children meet in the morning at _____ , and in the afternoon at _____ o'clock.
3. The school hours are from 9 to 12, and 2 to 5, in the summer; and from 9 to 12, and 2 to 4, in the winter.
4. The children must be sent to school clean and neat in person and dress.
5. No child may stay away from school without leave from the Master.
6. Leave of absence will readily be granted, either by application personally or by note: this application must be made before, and not after, the child absents itself.
7. If any child come late or be absent, a ticket of suspension will be sent, requiring a reason from the parent.
8. If the ticket be disregarded, the child will not be allowed to attend the school until a satisfactory answer has been given by the parent.
9. Every child must bring _____ a week, to be paid in advance every Monday morning: if there should be three children in one family desirous of attending school, the third will be admitted free.
10. No child will be admitted under the age of six years.
    N.B. No child will be admitted until it has been vaccinated.

Sold at the National Society's Depository, Sanctuary, Westminster.

(Rules to be adopted by schools in association with the
National Society in the 1860s.)

Blessings

To be recited at the beginning of a school day:

> Thank you for the world so sweet,
> Thank you for the food we eat.
> Thank you for the birds that sing,
> Thank you God for everything.
> Amen

To be recited at the end of the school day:

> Lord keep us safe this night
> Secure from all our fears.
> May angels guard us while we sleep
> 'Til morning light appears.
> Amen

> Now our school is over
> Father hear our prayer.
> Bless and keep our dear ones
> Safe beneath thy care.
> Help us all to serve thee
> To be kind and true,
> And keep a loving, tender heart
> In all we say and do.
> Amen.

Victorian school rhymes

You will never be sorry
For using gentle words,
For doing your best,
For being kind to the poor,
For looking before leaping,
For thinking before speaking,
For doing what you can to make others happy.

(Anon.)

Why do drill?
Children who do drill,
Seldom are ill,
Seldom look pale,
Delicate and frail,
Seldom are sulky and
Seldom are spiteful
But always delightful.
So dears, I still
Beg you to drill.

(Jennet Humphrey,
Laugh and Learn, 1890)

Marching Rhyme

We march to our places,
With clean hands and faces,
And pay great attention
To all we are told.
For we know we shall never
Be happy and clever,
But learning is better
than silver and gold.

(Anon.)

Eton beating

As we were all flocking out of school at the end of early lesson,
I beheld [Neville] standing ruefully alone among some empty
forms. A cry arose behind me: 'Hullo! There's going to be a swish-
ing!' and a general rush was made towards the upper end of the
schoolroom.

In the Lower School floggings were public. Several dozens of
fellows clambered upon forms and desks to see Neville corrected,
and I got a front place. Two fellows deputed to act as 'holders down'
stood behind the block, and one of them held a birch of quite alarm-
ing size, which he handed to the Lower Master as the latter
stepped down from his desk.

[The rod] was nearly five feet long, having three feet of handle
and nearly two of bush. As Mr Carter grasped it and poised it in
the air, addressing a few words of rebuke to Neville, it appeared a
horrible instrument for whipping so small a boy with. Neville was
unbracing his nether garments – next moment, when he knelt on
the step of the block, and when the Lower Master inflicted upon his
person six cuts that sounded like the splashes of so many buckets
of water, I turned almost faint.

(Account by J. Brinsley-Richards, then aged ten,
in *Seven Years at Eton*, c. 1867)

Etiquette rhymes

Under the Window

You are going out to tea today,
  So mind how you behave;
Let all accounts I have of you
  Be pleasant ones I crave.

Don't spill your tea, or gnaw your bread,
  And don't tease one another;
And Tommy mustn't talk too much,
  Or quarrel with his brother.

Say 'If you please', and Thank you, Nurse';
  Come home at eight o'clock;
And, Fanny, pray be careful that
  You do not tear your frock.

Now, mind your manners, children five,
  Attend to what I say;
And then, perhaps, I'll let you go
  Again another day.

(Kate Greenaway, 1879)

Whole Duty of Children

A child should always say what's true,
And speak when he is spoken to,
And behave mannerly at table:
At least as far as he is able

(Robert Louis Stevenson)

Miscellaneous rhymes

Preparing for Sunday

Haste! Put your playthings all away,
Tomorrow is the Sabbath Day.
Come bring to me your Noah's Ark,
Your pretty tinkling music cart:
Because my love, you must not play,
But holy keep the Sabbath Day.

(Anon.)

Solomon Grundy,
Born on Monday,
Christened on Tuesday,
Married on Wednesday,
Took ill on Thursday,
Worse on Friday,
Died on Saturday,
Buried on Sunday,
This is the end
Of Solomon Grundy.

(Rhyme used by Victorians
to teach children
the days of the week)

Worry not over the future,
The present is all thou hast,
The future will soon be the present,
And the present will soon be the past.

Miscellaneous rhymes
(continued)

Victorian rhyme

If I'm in heaven and you're not there
I'll carve your name on the golden chair
For all the angels there to see
I love you and you love me.
And if you're not there by judgement day
I'll know you've gone the other way
So just to prove my love is true
I'll go to hell just to be with you.

I am a Gold Lock

(Ask a friend to repeat each line after you)

I am a gold lock.
I am a gold key.

I am a silver lock.
I am a silver key.

I am a brass lock.
I am a brass key.

I am a lead lock.
I am a lead key.

I am a monk lock.
I am a monk key!

(Traditional)

Miscellaneous rhymes

(continued)

Charity

While once in haste I crossed the street,
    A little girl I saw,
Deep in the mud she'd placed her feet,
    And gazed on me with awe.

'Dear Sir,' with trembling tone she said,
    'Here have I stood for weeks,
And never had a bit of bread,'
    Her tears bedewed her cheeks.

'Poor child!' said I, 'do you stand here,
    And quickly I will buy
Some wholesome bread and strengthening beer,
    And fetch it speedily.'

Off ran I to the baker's shop,
    As hard as I could pelt,
Fearing t'was late, I made a stop,
    And in my pocket felt.

In my left pocket did I seek,
    To see how time went on,
Then grief and tears bedewed my cheek,
    For oh! my watch was gone!

(Lewis Carroll, 1832–98)

Miscellaneous rhymes

(continued)

Windy Nights

Whenever the moon and stars are set,
   Whenever the wind is high,
All night long in the dark and wet
   A man goes riding by.
Late in the night when the fires are out,
Why does he gallop and gallop about?

Whenever the trees are crying aloud,
   And ships are tossed at sea,
By on the highway, low and loud,
   By at the gallop goes he.
By at the gallop he goes, and then
By he comes back at the gallop again.

(Robert Louis Stevenson, 1850–1894)

How to write a letter

Maria intended to write a letter,
But could not begin (as she thought) to indite;
So went to her mother with pencil and slate,
Containing 'Dear Sister', and also a date.

'With nothing to say, my dear girl, do not think
Of wasting your time over paper and ink;
But certainly this is an excellent way
To try with your slate to find something to say.

'I will give you a rule,' said her mother, 'my dear,
Just think for a moment your sister is here,
And what would you tell her? Consider, and then,
Though silent your tongue, you can speak with your pen.'

(Elizabeth Turner, 1775–1846)

The little chimney sweep

Once upon a time there was a little chimney sweep, and his name was Tom. He lived in a great town in the North country, where there were plenty of chimneys to sweep, and plenty of money for Tom to earn and his master to spend. He could not read or write, and did not care to do either; and he never washed himself, for there was no water up the court where he lived . . .

(One day Tom climbs down a chimney and finds himself in a white room.)

The room was all dressed in white: white window curtains, white bed curtains, white furniture, and white walls, with just a few lines of pink here and there. The carpet was all over with gay little flowers and the walls were hung with pictures in gilt frames, which amused Tom very much . . .

The next thing he saw, and that too puzzled him, was a washing-stand, with ewers and basins, and soap and brushes, and towels; and a large bath, full of clean water – what a heap of things all for washing! 'She must be a very dirty lady,' thought Tom, 'by my master's rule, to want so much scrubbing as all that. But she must be very cunning to put the dirt out of the way so well afterwards, for I don't see a speck about the room, not even on the very towels.'

And then looking towards the bed, he saw that dirty lady, and held his breath with astonishment.

Under the snow-white coverlet, upon a snow-white pillow, lay the most beautiful girl Tom had ever seen . . .

(Tom then sees his reflection in the mirror.)

. . . And Tom, for the first time in his life, found out that he was dirty: and burst into tears with shame and anger; and turned to sneak up the chimney again and hide, and upset the fender, and threw the fire-irons down, with a noise as of ten thousand tin kettles tied to a thousand mad dogs' tails.

Up jumped the little white lady in her bed . . .

(from *The Water Babies* by Charles Kingsley)

Child labour

'For oh,' say the children, 'we are weary
   And we cannot run or leap;
If we cared for any meadows, it were merely
   To drop down in them and sleep.
Our knees tremble sorely in the stooping,
   We fall upon our faces, trying to go;
And underneath our heavy eyelids drooping
   The reddest flower would look as pale as snow.
For, all day, we drag our burden tiring
   through the coal-dark, underground;
Or, all day, we drive the wheels of iron
   In the factories, round and round.

For all day the wheels are droning, turning;
   Their wind comes in our faces,
Till our hearts turn, our heads with pulses burning,
   And the walls turn in their places:
Turns the sky in the high window, blank and reeling,
   Turns the long light that drops adown the wall,
Turns the black flies that crawl along the ceiling:
   All are turning, all the day, and we with all.
And all day, the iron wheels are droning,
   And sometimes we could pray,
'Oh ye wheels' (breaking out in a mad moaning)
   'Stop! be silent for to-day!'

(from 'Child Labour', Elizabeth Barrett Browning)

Our Mutual Friend

'It's my belief you hate the sight of the very river.'

'I–I do not like it, father.'

'As if it wasn't your living! As if it wasn't meat and drink to you!'

At these latter words the girl shivered again, and for a moment paused in her rowing, seeming to turn deadly faint. It escaped his attention, for he was glancing over the stern at something the boat had in tow.

'How can you be so thankless to your best friend, Lizzie? The very fire that warmed you when you were a baby, was picked out of the river alongside the coal barges. The very basket that you slept in, the tide washed ashore. The very rockers that I put it upon to make a cradle of it, I cut a piece of wood that drifted from some ship or another.'

(Lizzie's actual fear is of the dead man beng pulled behind their boat.)

'No. Has a dead man any use for money? Is it possible for a dead man to have money? What world does a dead man belong to? T'other world. What world does money belong to? This world. How can money be a corpse's? Can a corpse own it, want it, spend it, claim it, miss it?'

(From *Our Mutual Friend* by Charles Dickens)

Many happy hours

Building blocks are among the most
pleasing and instructive toys
ever invented for children.

The structures provide many happy
hours for boys and girls, do not readily
fall apart, and can be carried about

Children do not soon become tired of
the blocks, as their ingenuity is con-
stantly being called into exercise.

(Advertisement, England, 1879)

Victorian street rhymes

God made the bees,
The bees make the honey,
We do all the dirty work,
And teachers make the money.

Tommy broke a bottle
And blamed it on me.
I told Ma,
Ma told Pa,
Tommy got a whacking
on his Oom pa pa!

Eaver Weaver, chimney sweeper
Had a wife and couldn't keep her,
Had another, didn't love her,
Up the chimney he did shove her.

The Grace Darling Song

Grace Darling was born in Bamburgh in 1815. She lived on the Farne Islands, off the coast of Northumberland. Her father was keeper of the Longstone Lighthouse. On 7 September 1838, a paddle-steamer, the *Forfarshire*, was wrecked in a storm. Many of the people on board had drowned but some were clinging to a rock. In fierce seas, Grace helped her father to launch their small rowing boat and rescue the survivors. Nine people were saved and Grace became a national heroine. Artists arrived to paint her portrait, the national papers wrote of her daring deed and plays were performed about her exploit. Grace was bemused by such fame. Four years later she died of tuberculosis. The song is taken from a leaflet in the Grace Darling Museum, Bamburgh, Northumberland.

T'was on the Longstone Lighthouse,
There dwelt an English maid;
Pure as the air around her,
Of danger ne'er afraid.
One morning just at daybreak,
A storm-tossed wreck she spied:
And tho' to try seemed madness,
'I'll save the crew!' she cried.

Chorus:
And she pulled away, o'er the rolling sea,
Over the waters blue.
'Help! Help!' she could hear the cry
Of the shipwrecked crew.
But Grace had an English heart,
And the raging storm she braved;
She pulled away mid the dashing spray,
And the crew were saved.

The Grace Darling Song

(continued)

They to the rocks were clinging,
A crew of nine all told;
Between them and the lighthouse,
The sea like mountains rolled.
Said Grace, 'Come help me father
We'll launch that boat,' said she.
Her father cried: 'T'is madness,
To face that raging sea!'

(Chorus)

One murmured prayer 'Heaven guard us!'
And then they were afloat;
Between them and destruction,
The planks of that frail boat.
Then spoke the maiden's father:
'Return or doomed are we.'
But up spoke brave Grace darling:
'Alone I'll brave the sea.'

(Chorus)

They bravely rode the billows,
And reached the rock at length:
They saved the storm-tossed sailors,
In Heaven alone their strength.
Go, tell the wide world over
What English pluck can do;
And sing of brave Grace Darling
Who nobly saved the crew.

(Anon.)

Queen Victoria to
Miss Florence Nightingale

Windsor Castle (January) 1856

Dear MISS NIGHTINGALE

You are, I know, well aware of the high sense I entertain of the Christian devotion which you have displayed during this great and bloody war, and I need hardly repeat to you how warm my admiration is for your services, which are fully equal to those of my dear and brave soldiers, whose sufferings you have had the privilege of alleviating in so merciful a manner. I am, however, anxious of marking my feelings in a manner which I trust will be agreeable to you, and therefore send you with this letter a brooch, the form and emblems of which commemorate your great and blessed work, and which, I hope, you will wear as a mark of the high approbation of your Sovereign.

It will be a very great satisfaction to me, when you return at last to these shores, to make the acquaintance of one who has set so bright an example to our sex. And with every prayer for the preservation of your valuable health, believe me, always, yours sincerely,

VICTORIA R.

(The presentation took place on 29 January. The jewel resembled a badge rather than a brooch, bearing St George's Cross in red enamel, and the Royal cypher surmounted by a crown in diamonds. The inscription 'Blessed are the Merciful' encircled the badge, which also bore the word 'Crimea'.)

The Charge of the Light Brigade

Half a league, half a league,
Half a league onward,
All in the valley of Death
Rode the six hundred.
'Forward the Light Brigade!
Charge for the guns!' he said.
Into the valley of Death
Rode the six hundred.

'Forward, the Light Brigade!'
Was there a man dismay'd?
Not tho' the soldier knew
Some one had blunder'd.
Theirs not to make reply,
Theirs not to reason why,
Theirs but to do and die.
Into the valley of Death
Rode the six hundred.

Cannon to right of them,
Cannon to left of them,
Cannon in front of them
Volley'd and thunder'd;
Storm'd at with shot and shell,
Boldly they rode and well,
Into the jaws of Death,
Into the mouth of hell
Rode the six hundred.

Flash'd all their sabres bare,
Flash'd as they turn'd in air
Sabring the gunners there,

The Charge of the Light Brigade

(continued)

Charging an army, while
All the world wonder'd.
Plunged in the battery-smoke
Right thro' the line they broke;
Cossack and Russian
Reel'd from the sabre-stroke
Shatter'd and sunder'd.
Then they rode back, but not,
Not the six hundred.

Cannon to right of them,
Cannon to left of them,
Cannon behind them
Volley'd and thunder'd;
Storm'd at with shot and shell,
While horse and hero fell,
They that had fought so well
Came thro' the jaws of Death,
Back from the mouth of hell,
All that was left of them,
Left of six hundred.

When can their glory fade?
O the wild charge they made!
All the world wonder'd.
Honour the charge they made!
Honour the Light Brigade,
Noble six hundred!

(Alfred Lord Tennyson, c. 1880)

The Tay Bridge Disaster

Beautiful Railway Bridge of the Silv'ry Tay!
Alas! I am very sorry to say
That ninety lives have been taken away
On the last Sabbath day of 1879,
Which will be remember'd for a very long time.

'Twas about seven o'clock at night,
And the wind it blew with all its might,
And the rain came pouring down,
And the dark clouds seem'd to frown,
And the Demon of the air seem'd to say –
'I'll blow down the Bridge of Tay.'

When the train left Edinburgh
The passengers' hearts were light and felt no sorrow,
But Boreas blew a terrific gale
Which made their hearts for to quail,
And many of the passengers with fear did say –
'I hope God will send us safe across the Bridge of Tay.'

But when the train came near to Wormit Bay,
Boreas he did long and angry bay,
And shook the central girders of the Bridge of Tay
On the last Sabbath day of 1879,
Which will be remember'd for a very long time.

So the train sped on with all its might,
and Bonnie Dundee soon hove in sight,
And the passengers' hearts felt light,
Thinking they would enjoy themselves on the New Year,
With their friends at home they lov'd most dear,
And wish them all a Happy New Year.

The Tay Bridge Disaster

(continued)

So the train mov'd slowly across the Bridge of Tay,
Until it was about midway,
Then the central girders with a crash gave way,
And down went the train and passengers into the Tay!
The Storm Fiend did loudly bray,
Because ninety lives had been taken away,
On the last Sabbath day of 1879,
Which will be remember'd for a very long time.

As soon as the catastrophe came to be known
The alarm from mouth to mouth was blown,
And the cry rang out all o'er the town,
Good Heavens! the Tay Bridge is blown down,
And a passenger train from Edinburgh,
Which fill'd all the people's hearts with sorrow,
And made them for to turn pale,
Because none of the passengers were sav'd to tell the tale
How the disaster happen'd on the last Sabbath day of 1879,
Which will be remember'd for a very long time.

It must have been an awful sight,
To witness in the dusky moonlight,
While the Storm Fiend did laugh, and angry did bray,
Along the Railway Bridge of the Silv'ry Tay.
Oh! ill-fated bridge of the Silv'ry Tay,
I must now conclude my lay
By telling the world fearlessly without the least dismay,
That your central girders would not have given way,
At least many sensible men do say,
had they been supported on each side with buttresses,
At least many sensible men confesses,
For the stronger we our houses do build,
The less chance we have of being killed.

(William McGonagall, 1830–1902)

Notes on anthology selections

Dotheboys Hall (p. 56)

Children can devise a prospectus for Dotheboys Hall, one which attempts to persuade the rich to part with large sums of money for the education of their sons. They may, of course, need to be a little 'economical with the truth', glossing over the faults and describing instead some of the many and varied attractions that the school has to offer. The extract from *Nicholas Nickleby* shows the reality of school life, and children will need to consider how they can feature the school in a positive light.

Rules . . . (p. 58)

How do these compare with school rules today? What would be the most common reasons for absence from school or for being late for school in Victorian times? How would these compare with the reasons given today? Children could compose a note to school as if from a Victorian parent, requesting leave of absence or explaining why their child was late for school.

Victorian school rhymes (p. 60)

Children could try rote-learning these in the way that Victorian children would do. Remind them that children would often be slapped over the knuckles with a ruler if they went wrong!

Eton beating (p. 61)

Many Victorian children became familiar with violent behaviour when they were sent to school. Boys from rich families were often sent away to school from the age of seven where as the 'servants' of older boys they would suffer much corporal punishment. This extract is a particularly gruesome account. Children could write a diary entry for the day of the beating from the perspective of one of the 'holders down' or the master's report in the punishment book.

Etiquette rhymes

'Under the Window' (p. 62)

'Whole Duty of Children' (p. 62)

These poems could lead to a discussion about manners. In Victorian times many adults believed that, in adult company children should only speak when spoken to. What are children's views on this today? How important are manners? Do they believe that 'Manners maketh man'?

Miscellaneous rhymes

'Preparing for Sunday' (p. 63)

In many households, Sunday was a day for going to church. The only book to be read was the Bible and the only toys to be played with were those that taught children about the Bible, such as Noah's Arks. To many children Sundays were very long and very boring days. How would children cope with this sort of day in the twenty-first century?

'I am a Gold Lock' (p. 64)
The sort of puzzle poem that children loved to trick each other with.

'Charity' (p. 65)
Lewis Carroll was a pseudonym for Charles Lutwidge Dodgson. His most famous books were *Alice's Adventures in Wonderland* and *Through the Looking Glass*, which included the nonsense poem 'Jabberwocky' along with 'Father William' and 'The Walrus and the Carpenter'. Children could undertake an author study on Lewis Carroll.

The poem 'Charity' tells of a theft by a pickpocket, and children could be asked to compile the police report of the incident.

'Windy Nights' (p. 66)
Robert Louis Stevenson (1850–94) is probably best known for his fiction. *Treasure Island* and *Kidnapped* were popular titles. In 1885 his poetry was collected into *A Child's Garden of Verse* which is widely regarded as one of the best books of poetry ever written for children. Question children as to why the man goes riding by in 'Windy Nights'. Where is he going, and why is he back so soon?

How to write a letter (p. 67)
How many children find it hard to write letters these days? They did in Victorian times too!

The little chimney sweep (p. 68)
In this extract from *The Water Babies*, Tom, the chimney sweep, loses his way in the chimney flues of an old country house and finds himself in a room, '. . . the like of which he had never seen before'. As he takes in what he sees, he glimpses in the mirror 'a little ugly, black, ragged figure . . .' and realises that he is looking at his reflection. At that point the occupant of the bedroom, a young girl, wakes up. Ask children to predict what both characters do next. Can they write their own suggestions for the story's next paragraph and then compare them to Charles Kingsley's original? What sort of room would Tom be used to sleeping in? How would it compare with the room that he finds himself in?

Child labour (p. 69)
Elizabeth Barrett Browning wrote a lengthy poem 'The Cry of the Children' which was an outburst against the employment of young children in factories. In 1846 she married the poet Robert Browning.

Our Mutual Friend (p. 70)
In London, the River Thames proved useful to the poor. Dickens' novel *Our Mutual Friend* begins with gaffer Hexam and his daughter rowing a boat on the Thames in search of dead bodies. These would then be taken in tow and handed over to the police, but not before any money or valuables had been removed from the corpse.

Read children the extract from the book and consider Lizzie's feelings about the job that she does with her father. How do children feel about Gaffer's justification for robbing a dead man?

Dickens sets the scene at twilight and writes further on of, '. . . a tender yellow moonlight on the water'. Can children describe the mood of the river at this time of day, thinking about words and phrases for the flow of the water, the colours of the sky, the effects of moonlight and the night noises that can be heard?

Victorian street rhymes (p. 72)

Further examples may be found in books by the Opies, Peter and Iona, who collected material on the folklore of childhood.

The Grace Darling Song (p. 73)

This is a great piece for recitation as part of an assembly production: lots of oilskin coats as costumes, a few lanterns, a darkened hall, some rough sea sound effects and a class of children belting out the chorus.

Queen Victoria to Miss Florence Nightingale (p. 75)

After reading this and considering its regal tones, children might care to compose a reply. How do you write to a Queen? What would be the most appropriate language?

The Charge of the Light Brigade (p. 76)

This poem was written about a fatal mistake during the Crimean War against Russia (1853–56). When British horse soldiers were ordered to charge the Russian guns it proved to be a suicidal attempt.

Ask children for comments on the rhythm of the poem (strong, pounding, echoing the thunder of the cannons and the horses' hooves).

What do children notice about the rhymes? Is there a regular rhyming pattern? Point out the pattern of triple lines that rhyme and that others have half-rhymes or near rhymes that echo each other: hundred/thunder'd.

Children could consider how the poem might be arranged for group presentation. Where would the poem be divided up for different voices? How should the different parts be read? Which parts need to be spoken more loudly or more softly than others? Are there appropriate actions or sound effects which would add something to the performance?

The Tay Bridge Disaster (p. 78)

William McGonagall (1830–1902) was a Scottish poet who wrote poems which were recognised to be uniformly bad. Children could be asked to consider why a poem such as this was labelled bad. Pay particular attention to the somewhat forced rhythm and rhyme, and the prosaic quality of the final third of the poem.

Children could also research the disaster and write a newspaper account of what happened.